Learn Paradox 4.5 in a Day

For Version 4.5 for DOS

Timothy Colman

Wordware Publishing, Inc.

ISBN 1-55622-419-2

10 9 8 7 6 5 4 3 2 1

9407

Paradox is a registered trademark of Borland International, Inc.
PC-DOS is a registered trademark of International Business Machines Corporation.
MS-DOS and Xenix are registered trademarks of Microsoft Corporation.
Other product names mentioned are used for identification purposes only and may be trademarks of their
respective companies.

All inquiries for volume purchases of this book should be addressed to Wordware
Publishing, Inc., at the above address. Telephone inquiries may be made by calling:

(214) 423-0090

Contents

Section 1

Introduction

This book is designed to be completed in a short period of time. It should take you about one day to finish. The best way to use this book is to sit down with your computer and work through the exercises. For best results, read the book from beginning to end.

This book is designed for persons familiar with the basic operation of a personal computer but who have no prior experience with Paradox. Although this book is based on Paradox Version 4.5, the majority of commands discussed will also work in Version 4.0 of Paradox. Therefore, wherever you see a reference to Paradox 4.5, this reference will also apply to Paradox 4.0 unless otherwise noted.

Objectives

The objective of this book is to teach you to use the Paradox 4.5 commands necessary to manage a simple database system.

When you have completed the exercises in this book, you will be able to:

- Create a Paradox 4.5 table
- Add to and edit the contents of a table
- View a single table or multiple tables
- Rearrange the information in tables
- Query Paradox tables
- Create reports from tables
- Record and play back Paradox 4.5 scripts
- Display simple Paradox 4.5 graphs

This book does not address the powerful programming language that comes with Paradox 4.5. Discussion of this advanced feature of Paradox 4.5 is beyond the scope of this book. The Paradox Application Language (PAL) is addressed in the book *Learn PAL in a Day*, also from Wordware Publishing, Inc.

Throughout the book, exercises refer to using Paradox 4.5 either from the keyboard or with a mouse. You are always provided with both methods so that if you do not have a mouse with your PC you can still complete the exercise. Use of a mouse is recommended but is not necessary to complete the exercises in this book.

To assist you in the successful completion of this book, a data disk is included in the package. This disk contains all the sample files used in the book.

Section 2

What is Paradox 4.5?

```
▦  View  Ask  Report  Create  Modify  Image  Forms  Tools  Scripts  Exit
                                   Customer
CUSTOMER│Cust ID│ First Name  │ MI │  Last Name  │           Address
    1   │ 1001  │Mary         │ R  │Walker       │907 Ponds Court
    2   │ 1002  │Walter       │ A  │Dinkins      │8200 Southwestern
    3   │ 1003  │Allison      │ A  │Evans        │6201 Village Bend
    4   │ 1004  │Melissa      │ C  │Colman       │9452 E. Valley Ranch
    5   │ 1005  │Carole       │ D  │Terrell      │1 Greenpeace Way
    6   │ 1006  │Bob          │ M  │Nichols      │1000 N. Central
    7   │ 1007  │Betty        │ B  │McIntire     │555 Canal Street
    8   │ 1008  │Jim          │ T  │Cannon       │417 Longwood
┌[▪]                              Inven                                 [↑]┐
INVEN │Stock Num│      Title        │    Description    │        Cost
    1 │  0001   │History of Ireland │The Last 300 Years │     20.00
    2 │  0002   │Hang-Gliding Basics│Fly without crashing│     6.00
    3 │  0003   │Romance in the Snow│Snow Bunnies in Love│     5.00
    4 │  0004   │Travel Adventures  │Low Cost Travelling│      8.00
    5 │  0005   │Sailing the Atlantic│Across in a 32' Boat│     7.00
    6 │  0006   │How to Jump Rope   │Hop, Skip, Jump    │     3.00
    7 │  0007   │Paradox 4.0 In A Day│Easy to Learn     │      9.00
    8 │  0008   │Car Buyers Guide   │1995 Model Year    │     3.00
    9 │  0009   │Fairy Tales for Kids│Tales from Grimm  │      4.00
        8 of 10                  ◄▪
F1 Help   F7 Form   Alt-F9 CoEdit                            Main
```

Paradox 4.5 is an easy-to-use database program. It is a powerful program, able to perform rapid searches and produce sophisticated reports. Programs with these virtues traditionally have been difficult to learn and use. The goal of the designers of Paradox 4.5 was to make a powerful program that was easy to learn and use.

To reach this goal, Paradox 4.5 uses a series of pull-down menus. You carry out powerful operations by making selections from the menus that Paradox displays. These operations can work with multiple sources of information (called "tables") and can display results using customized screen formats.

Paradox 4.5 does not require programming skills to use it effectively. It does, however, include a programming language that can be used to create custom database applications designed around your particular needs.

Reports can be created easily and stored for later use. Information extracted from several tables can be linked and displayed in many ways, including useful business graphs.

Paradox can effectively perform mathematics on tables of information, but its best use is in sorting and searching operations. Lotus 1-2-3 is a more effective number-crunching program than Paradox 4.5, but Paradox is much better at capturing tabular information. Further, Paradox has a great advantage over programs like Lotus 1-2-3 in its ability to build complex reports linking information across multiple tables.

Section 3

Setting the Scene

In this book, you build a simple customer information system for your company. Your imaginary company sells books. Your customers are a diverse group from all over the country. Many of them have ordered books from you several times. How can Paradox 4.5 help you to manage the business?

Think about the requirements for servicing your customers. You need to communicate with your customers, keep track of inventory, and track all financial information. Paradox 4.5 will help you by capturing information in all of these areas.

Specifically, what information do you need to capture about *customers*? Consider these possibilities:

Customer ID A unique identifier for each customer

First Name The customer's first name

Last Name The customer's last name

Address The street address of your customer

City The city in which your customer lives

State The state in which your customer lives

Zip Your customer's zip code

History Descriptive text about your customer

The reasons for capturing most of this information are obvious. However, the Customer ID field requires a bit of explanation. Each customer is assigned a unique number used to track key information about that customer. Information located in different Paradox tables can be linked by finding matching Customer ID numbers.

What kind of information do you need to store regarding your *book inventory*? Consider these items:

Stock Number Every title in inventory is given a unique stock number

Title   The title of the book

Description   A brief description of the book

Cost   The cost of the book to your business

Retail   The retail price of the book

On-Hand   The on-hand quantity of this book

The Stock Number is used to track all orders for a particular book.

What about information relating to *book orders*? Information on such transactions might include:

Customer ID   The number of the customer placing the order

Stock Number The stock number of the book being ordered

Quantity   The quantity being ordered

Date   The date of the book order

Notice that the Customer ID and the Stock Number are repeated pieces of information. By capturing the customer number in two places, you can easily pull related pieces of data from both sources. The same is true of the stock number. Using the stock number, you can pull out information on title, description, cost and retail from one source and order quantities and order dates from another source.

Now that you know what kinds of information you need to track, you next install the program. The remainder of this book shows you how to use the features of Paradox 4.5 to efficiently manage your customer information.

Section 4

Installing Paradox 4.5

Paradox 4.5 comes with an easy-to-use installation program. To install the program with all of its optional software requires about 5.3 megabytes on your hard disk.

Before you begin the installation process, make complete copies of all the diskettes that came with your Paradox 4.5 package. Use the copies during installation. Store the original program diskettes in a safe place.

Throughout this section, we will assume you are installing Paradox 4.5 on disk drive C using floppy disks in disk drive A. If you wish, you can install the program on any available hard disk.

1. Power on your computer system. When the machine has completed the startup process, make sure the DOS prompt for your hard disk is displayed:

   C:\>

   If another drive prompt is displayed, type **C:** and press **Enter**.

2. Place the **Paradox Disk 1 (of 2)** in drive A. The next command you type will depend on whether you have a color or a monochrome monitor.

   If you have a color monitor, type the command:

   A:INSTALL

   In you have a monochrome monitor, type the command:

   A:INSTALL -B&W

   After typing the command, press **Enter**.

   The second version of the command causes Paradox 4.5 to take best advantage of your monochrome monitor.

3. The Paradox 4.5 installation program starts, displaying a screen like this one.

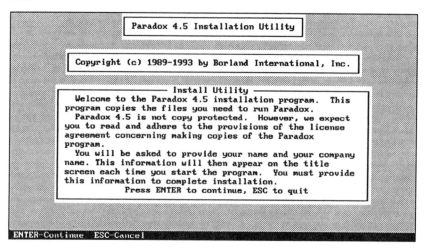

4. Read the message on this screen. When you are ready to proceed, press **Enter**.

   Paradox asks you to verify the source drive (drive A in this example). Press **Enter**. From the next screen, select the option:

   Standalone installation

   Press **Enter**.

   Next, the installation program displays a screen requesting several pieces of information, as shown:

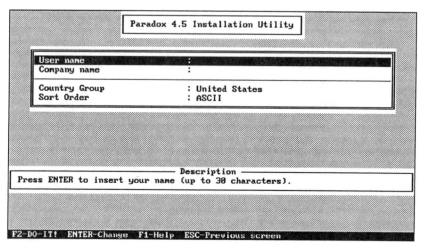

5. Press **Enter**. The installation program places a box on the screen into which you type your name. After typing your name, press **Enter** again.

   Move to the next line and enter a company name, then press **Enter** to continue.

   The lower portion of installation screen displays two pieces of information you should not have to change. The Country Group selection tells Paradox 4.5 how to display currency figures, time formats, and other values that vary from country to country. The Sort Order selection specifies the way in which Paradox carries out sorts.

6. After typing the name and serial number information, press the function key **F2**. This is the DO-IT! key, and it tells Paradox you have completed this step and are ready to proceed.

   The next screen in the installation program asks you to specify the installation directory, and whether to install optional files.

   Unless you specify another one, Paradox 4.5 installs itself in the **C:\PDOX45** subdirectory. For the purposes of this book it is recommended you use the default directory and install all the optional files. If the recommended subdirectory is suitable, press F2 to proceed.

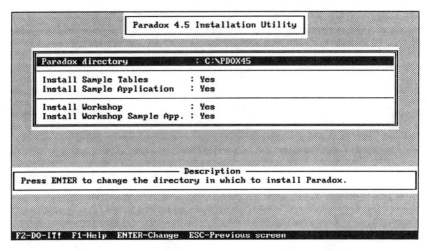

7. The installation program takes a moment to copy files, then it asks you to insert **Paradox Disk 2 (of 2)**. Insert this disk, then press any key to continue.

   A number of files are copied to your hard drive, then the installation program displays a message suggesting you register your Paradox software. This screen provides telephone numbers for registration, then asks you to press any key to exit.

Installation is complete. Press any key on your keyboard. Paradox returns to the DOS prompt, as shown below.

`C:\>b:install`

`C:\>`

Section 5

The Paradox 4.5 Table

The word *table* is used to refer to a collection of information that is stored in rows and columns. The rows are called *records* and the columns are called *fields*. A customer address record might consist of several fields: a first name field, a last name field, an address field, a city field, a state field, and so on. A collection of records is called a table in Paradox 4.5.

In the illustration below a typical Paradox 4.5 table is shown. Note the field names are displayed at the top of each column in the field. Along the left side of the screen the record numbers for the records in the table are displayed.

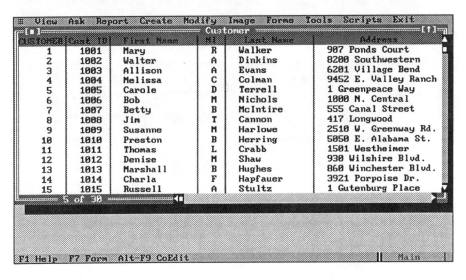

Section 6

Starting Paradox

Follow these steps to start Paradox 4.5:

1. From the DOS prompt, change to the Paradox 4.5 subdirectory.

   To do this, type **CD\PDOX45** and press **Enter**.

2. Now start the Paradox program.

   Type **PARADOX** and press **Enter**.

3. After the program is loaded, the Paradox screen appears as shown here:

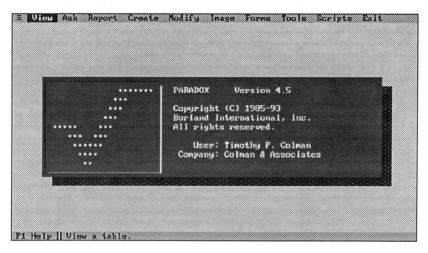

In the next section we discuss the different parts of the Paradox screen.

Section 7

The Paradox Screen

The opening Paradox screen is divided into three parts: the Main menu in a *menu bar* at the top of the screen, a *speed bar/status bar* at the bottom of the screen, and the Paradox *desktop* between these two. Sometimes Paradox also displays a *message area* in the lower right corner of the screen. In the illustration, note the position of the *menu bar*, the *speed bar/status bar*, the *desktop* and the *message area*.

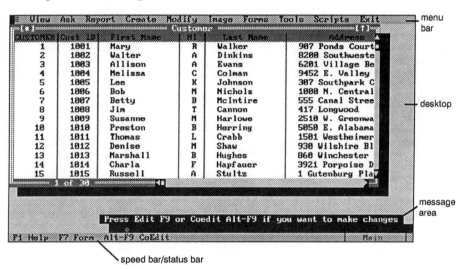

The Main menu always appears at the top of the screen. Frequently, Paradox will also display informational messages here. These messages are designed to tell you how to proceed to the next step in a command. Try to read and understand these messages completely.

13

The desktop area of the screen is where the information from a table will appear. It is the largest part of the screen.

The speed bar/status bar at the bottom of the screen contains shortcut commands that can be executed by clicking with a mouse. It also displays status information about operations carried out on the desktop.

The message area is the place where Paradox occasionally displays status messages. It will always appear in the lower right corner of the screen.

More about the Main menu follows.

Section 8

The Main Menu

When you start Paradox, the Main menu appears above the desktop at the top of the screen. This menu consists of one row of options and a series of pull-down menus. When a command on the Main menu is highlighted, descriptive information about the highlighted command appears in the status bar at the bottom of the screen.

For example, when the View option is highlighted, as in the previous illustration, Paradox displays the descriptive phrase "View a table" in the status bar. Similarly, if the Report option is highlighted, Paradox displays the descriptive phrase "Output, design, or change a report specification."

Briefly, the Paradox menu options do the following:

▦	This is the System menu option. It modifies the appearance of the desktop.
View	Display a table on the screen.
Ask	Select data from the table, perform calculations with this data.
Report	Design, modify, and print reports from one or more tables.
Create	Build new table structures.
Modify	Add information, edit information, and sort information in a table. Also modify the structure, or arrangement, of information in the table.
Image	Rearrange information on the screen, display graphs, and display cross-tabs.
Forms	Create or modify data entry forms.

Tools   Rename tables, copy tables, carry out DOS commands, and many other useful operations.

Scripts   Record a series of commands, then play them back to "automate" operations in Paradox.

Exit   Leave Paradox.

Note also the message in the status bar: *F1 Help*. A comprehensive Help system is built into Paradox. To access this Help system at any time, press F1 or click on this option with your mouse.

Options can be selected from the Main menu in three ways.

- Highlight the desired option and press Enter.
- Press the first letter of the selected option.
- Click on the desired option with the mouse

This command selection method works on all menus in Paradox 4.5. In the following examples, you can use any method to execute commands.

The Main menu is not always active, even when it is displayed on the screen. For example, after displaying a table with the View command, Paradox does not automatically reactivate the menu. If the Main menu is active, a colored highlight will appear on the screen. If the highlight is not visible, it can be displayed by pressing the function key F10. Note that the *mode indicator* in the lower right corner of the screen dictates the kind of menu seen when you press F10. When the mode indicator displays Main, the Main menu appears. In other modes, like the Edit mode for example, a different menu is displayed.

One new element of Paradox 4.5 is its compatibility with a mouse. In nearly every situation where you select commands, you may use either the keyboard or the mouse to make your selection. In the following exercises you may also use either method. Understand that when selecting an option from a menu, it is *not* necessary to press F10 first. Simply click on the desired option.

Section 9

The Help System

Paradox contains a built-in Help system. The Help system contains a file of in-depth information on a broad range of topics in Paradox, from simple to complex.

There are two ways to access the Help system: by pressing the function key **F1**, or by clicking on the F1 Help option in the speed bar. In the following example you use both methods.

1. Activate the Help system by pressing the function key:

   F1

   Paradox displays a help screen, as shown below. The actual contents of the Help screen will vary depending on what you were doing when you asked for help. Paradox is sensitive to your command selections and displays information relevant to the most recently selected commands.

```
 Basics  GettingAround  Keys  MenuChoices  Index  Scripts/PAL  Paradox
 ──────────────────── About the Paradox Help System ────────────────────

    ◆ The double-line border tells you that you're in the Help System.
      Note that the Paradox menu has been replaced by the Help System menu.

    ◆ Press [F1] at any time during a Paradox session.  The Help System
      gives you information about what you were doing when you pressed [F1].

    ◆ Browse the Help System by making Help menu selections.

    ◆ Once you're in the Help System, press [F1] again to get the index.
      (Choose Index from the menu above for more about how to use the index.)

    ◆ While you're in the Help System, press [Esc] to return to the
      previous help screen or back to Paradox.

    ◆ Choose Paradox or Back from the Help System menu to return to
      Paradox.



      Choose a help menu item.  [F1] for help index.  Paradox to resume.

 F1 Index │ Basic Paradox terms and concepts.
```

2. Notice that the Help system displays a menu much like the Main menu at the top of the screen. You can make selections from the menu by pressing the first letter of the option, or by highlighting the desired option and pressing **Enter,** or by clicking on the desired option with your mouse.

Note the Help option called Paradox at the end of the menu. Present on all Help screens, this option returns to the Paradox screen being viewed before calling for help.

Highlight the option:

Paradox

Press **Enter.** Paradox returns to the Paradox desktop, with the Main menu active.

3. The Help system is *context-sensitive*, meaning it attempts to find helpful information about the command or operation currently in use.

Let's see how this works. From the Main menu, select the option:

Image

Paradox displays the Image pull-down menu, beginning with the option TableSize. This time select the Help system by clicking on the F1 Help option in the speed bar, or if you do not have a mouse, press the function key **F1**.

Paradox displays the Help screen shown below:

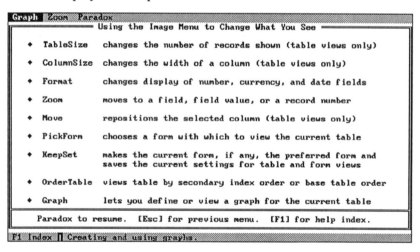

Note that Paradox displays a different Help screen, this one related to Image commands.

4. The Paradox 4.5 Help system also contains an extensive index of topics. Assume for a moment that you wanted information on the topic Tables. Use the Help index to find information on this topic.

At the bottom right of the Image command help screen is this selection:

[F1] for help index

Select this option by pressing the function key:

F1

Paradox displays the Help index, as shown below. This index begins with an overview of the Paradox Help system, then alphabetically lists a broad range of topics. The index contains hundreds of entries and is so lengthy that Paradox provides a method for searching through it rapidly.

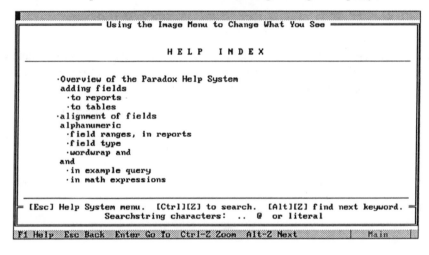

5. Notice the bottom center portion of the Help Index screen. The option Ctrl-Z allows you to search through the lengthy Help Index.

Tell Paradox to display topics related to Tables. To do this, press:

Ctrl-Z

6. Paradox displays a message on the status bar: **Enter value or pattern**.

A dialog box appears in the center of the screen. Into this dialog box type:

..tables..

Press **Enter**.

This entry uses wild cards (the periods in front of and behind the word "tables") to search for any entry in the Help index that contains the word **tables**.

7. Paradox jumps to the first entry in the Help index containing the word "tables." If the first topic found is not the one you want, you can tell Paradox to search for the next occurrence of the topic.

To find the next occurrence of the word "tables," press:

Alt-Z

Paradox skips to the next entry containing the word "tables." You may continue pressing Alt-Z until you locate the desired topic.

When you have reached the desired topic, press **Enter** to view the Help system information on this topic.

8. Now leave the Help system. To do this, select the option:

Paradox

Remember to press **Enter** if you are highlighting options instead of typing the first letter of an option.

Paradox returns to the desktop with the Main menu active. Because you selected the Image command before going into the Help system, Paradox returns to the desktop with this menu still visible.

9. Press **Esc** to clear the Image pull-down menu from the screen.

Section 10

Special Keys in Paradox 4.5

Throughout this book a number of function keys and other key combinations are frequently used. These "shortcuts" are summarized below.

F1	Help
F2	Do-It!
F3	Up-Image
F4	Down-Image
Alt-F5 or Ctrl-F	Field View
F6	Check Mark
F7	Form Toggle
Alt-F7	Instant Report
Ctrl-F7	Graph
F8	Clear Image
Alt-F8	Clear All
F9	Edit
F10	Menu

Section 11

Creating a Paradox Table

In the section entitled Setting the Scene, we identified the various kinds of information we want to capture in your Paradox 4.5 tables. In this exercise, create a table called Cust containing customer name and address information. This table captures the same information contained in the Customer table used in later exercises.

To create a table in Paradox, you provide a *table structure*. A table structure is a description of the information to be captured in the table. For example, your customer information table will have the following fields:

Customer ID   The unique customer number for each customer

First Name   The customer's first name

Last Name   The customer's last name

Address   The customer's street address

City   The city in which the customer resides

State   The state in which the customer resides

Zip Code   The zip code in which the customer resides

History   Descriptive text about the customer

When building the table structure you provide information about the *name* of each field, the field *type* and sometimes the field *size*, and whether or not the field is a *key field*.

The *name* of the field should describe its contents. For example, name the field that holds the first name of a customer **First Name**. The name can be up to 25 characters in length. It cannot begin with a space, but it may contain spaces.

The *field type* is a description of the kind of information to be stored in the field. For example, in the field list above note that some of the information is alphabetic, while other pieces of information are numeric. Use field types to distinguish one kind of information from another. In Paradox there are five commonly used field types. These five are the alphanumeric, numeric, currency, date, and memo field types. The Last Name field would be an alphanumeric field, while the Zip Code field would typically be a numeric field. If we recorded transaction amounts in this table, this information would be stored in a currency field. Transaction dates could be captured in a date field. Large amounts of text should be placed in a memo field. Only the alphanumeric field type and the memo field type require that you specify a size for the field.

When building the table structure you may elect to create a *key field*. A key field is used to identify records. A good candidate for a key field is the Customer ID field. To designate a field as a key field, place an asterisk next to its field type.

Designating the Customer ID field as a key field offers three advantages:

- *Sorts the table on the key field.* When you view this table, Paradox automatically displays the table sorted by Customer ID order.
- *Prevents duplicate keys.* If you try to post a new record using a Customer ID that already exists in the table, Paradox either replaces the earlier record with the same key, or it displays a key violation message in the message area.
- *Speeds searches of the table.* Paradox creates an index based on the key field. This index is used to speed queries of the table.

Key fields are optional but in many cases very helpful. For the sake of simplicity, in the next exercise we will not use key fields. The following table is a simple one, but it provides many opportunities to examine Paradox table commands.

1. At the end of the last exercise, you returned from the Help system to the Paradox 4.5 desktop. The Main menu should still be active. If it is not, press:

   [F10] Menu

   Your screen should look like the following illustration:

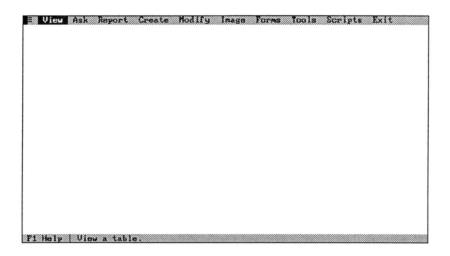

2. From the Main menu, select the command:

Create

Paradox displays a dialog box asking you to enter a table name. The table name can be no more than eight characters in length. Type the name:

CUST

Press **Enter**.

Paradox now displays a table definition screen.

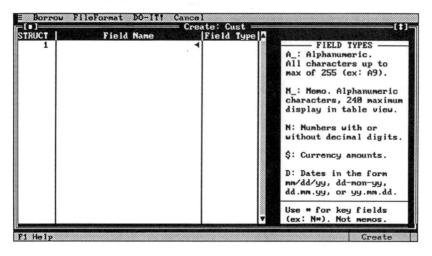

3. The table definition screen allows you to describe the elements of the Cust table. It also contains information about the different field types.

   The field types are:

A **Alphanumeric**	This field can contain letters, numbers, punctuation symbols, or any other character on your keyboard. Indicate this field type by entering **A** followed by a number. For example, **A25** tells Paradox to create an alphanumeric field 25 spaces in length.
M **Memo**	This field can also contain letters, numbers, punctuation symbols, or any other character on your keyboard. It is designed to hold large amounts of text; up to 64 megabytes of text can be stored in a single memo field. Indicate this field type by entering **M** followed by a number. The number indicates the *display length*, not the maximum number of characters which can be stored. For example, **M25** tells Paradox to create a memo field, with a display length of 25 characters.
N **Numbers**	This field type can contain any number up to 17 decimal positions in length, including decimal places.
$ **Currency**	Stores monetary numbers. Two decimal places are assumed, commas are placed in numbers, and negative numbers are placed in parentheses.
D **Dates**	This field captures date information in any of the following formats: **mm/dd/yy, dd-mm-yy,** or **dd.mm.yy**

   Now define the columns (or fields) of the table.

4. Define the first column of the table. With the cursor in the Field Name column, type the name:

   Customer ID

   Press **Right Arrow** to move to the Field Type column. Type the entry:

   A4

   This identifies the field as an alphanumeric field four spaces in length. Press **Enter** to move to the next row of the table description.

5. Move the cursor to the Field Name column, then type the entry:

   First Name

Press the **Right Arrow** to move to the Field Type column and type:

A12

This tells Paradox that the First Name field will contain a maximum of 12 characters of alphanumeric information (letters and numbers).

6. Continue entering field information to the table description screen. Add the fields described below:

Field Name	*Field Type*
Last Name	**A12**
Address	**A20**
City	**A15**
State	**A2**
Zip	**A5**
History	**M24**

When complete, your table description should look like this illustration.

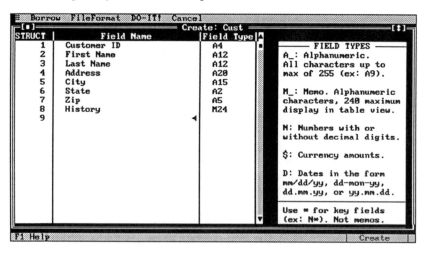

7. Now save the table description you have created. Press the key:

DO-IT! [F2]

Paradox displays the message "Creating Cust" in the message area of the desktop, then redisplays the desktop with the Main menu active.

Section 12

Copying Tables and Changing the Default Directory

In the last exercise, you created a simple customer information table. When you saved your work with the DO-IT! command (function key F2), where did Paradox 4.5 store your table? As a default setting, Paradox 4.5 stores your tables in the directory that contains the program, usually C:\PDOX45. With the Tools Copy Table command, you can duplicate your table onto a floppy disk.

With the Tools More Directory command, you can specify where Paradox 4.5 will store and retrieve your tables for the remainder of your Paradox session.

The Tools menu contains a number of useful commands, including the Export/Import command. This command allows you to import and export data from a range of other programs, including Lotus 1-2-3.

In this short exercise, you copy the Cust table to your floppy disk, then change the Paradox 4.5 default directory.

1. Place the floppy disk that accompanied this book in drive A. (Note: If your 5.25 inch disk drive is drive B, then use this drive instead of A.)

2. From the Main menu, select the option:

Tools

Paradox shows you the Tools pull-down menu. Take a moment to examine the list of tools displayed.

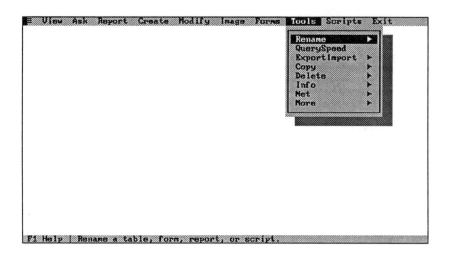

3. Highlight the **Copy** option. Note the descriptive phrase displayed in the status bar:

   Copy of a table, form, report, or script

   We will use the option to copy the Cust table to the diskette in drive A. Select the **Copy** command by pressing **Enter**.

4. Paradox displays a second pull-down menu, overlaying the first. From the this menu, select the option:

   Table

   Paradox 4.5 displays a dialog box asking you to enter a table name. This is the table you are copying *from*. Type the name **CUST** and press **Enter**.

   Paradox 4.5 asks for the name of the new table. Type:

   A:CUST

   This entry tells Paradox 4.5 to place a copy of CUST on drive A. By placing the destination path (A:\, B:\, etc.) in front of the table you can easily redirect the table to another drive.

   Press **Enter** to complete the command. Paradox 4.5 takes a few seconds to place a copy of the Cust table on your floppy disk, then redisplays the desktop.

5. Now we will tell Paradox 4.5 to save all future tables to your floppy disk.

   Select the command:

   Tools

As before, Paradox 4.5 displays a list of tools. Notice the option More. This option will display a second list of tools. Select:

More

Paradox displays a new pull-down menu, as shown:

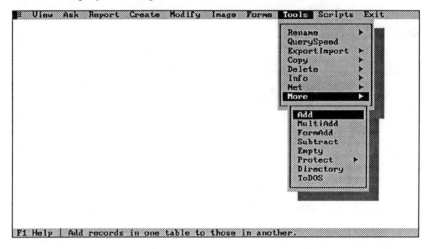

6. From this menu, the Directory option allows you to specify a default directory. This directory setting will remain in effect for the remainder of your Paradox session.

    Select:

    Directory

    Paradox 4.5 displays the current directory setting C:\PDOX45.

7. Use the **Backspace** key to remove the old directory setting. Type the new setting:

    A:

    Press **Enter**. Paradox 4.5 will now direct all files *to drive A*. It will also load all files *from drive A*.

    When the command is complete, Paradox 4.5 displays the Main menu with a message confirming your new directory setting.

Viewing Tables and Moving Between Tables

Use the View command to load a table onto the desktop. In this exercise, load the Cust table to the desktop, then a similar table called Customer.

1. Your screen should look like the illustration below. Note that the desktop is currently empty.

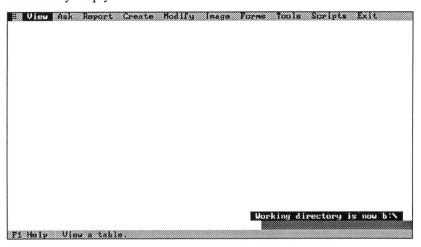

2. Select the command:

View

Paradox 4.5 asks you to enter a table name. Type the name:

CUST

Press **Enter**. Paradox reads the Cust file from your disk in drive A, then displays this file on the desktop. Note that Paradox tells you that the table is empty. You have not yet added any records to the table.

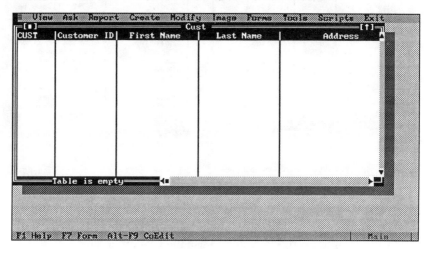

3. The View command allows you to load and examine more than one table at a time. In this step you load a second table. This second table will look similar to the Cust table, but it already contains a number of records. The way in which you select the file will also be improved.

   Note that the Main menu is not active. Press the **F10** function key to activate the Main menu.

   Select the command:

   View

4. Paradox displays a dialog box asking you to type in a table name. The majority of this dialog box is empty. Paradox can display a list of available table names in this dialog box. To see this list, press **Enter**.

   Paradox then shows you a list of available tables. Highlight the file named Customer.

   Press **Enter** or click on the **OK** button with your mouse.

   Paradox 4.5 loads the Customer table to the desktop, as shown below:

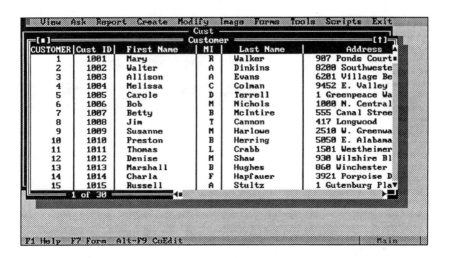

Notice the structure of the Customer table. It contains the same arrangement of information included in the Cust table. For most of the forthcoming exercises, you will use the Customer table.

5. Examine the appearance of the data in the Customer table by scrolling up and down, left and right within the table.

This arrangement of rows and columns has a name in Paradox 4.5. It is called the Table view.

The Table view is the default method for displaying data in Paradox 4.5. It displays fields as columns from left to right on the screen. Records are numbered down the left side of the screen. Later in this book we will also work with another view of Paradox 4.5 tables called the Forms view.

6. You now have two tables in the desktop: Cust and Customer. Although the Customer table is visible right now; if you look closely you can see the border of the Cust table at the top of the desktop.

How can you see the contents of Cust? Paradox provides a set of commands to help out. To move back and forth between tables in the desktop, Paradox provides the Up Image [F3] and the Down Image [F4] commands.

The Up Image [F3] command displays the previous table if more than one is on the desktop. The Down Image [F4] command displays the next table if more than one table is on the desktop.

Press the Up Image key:

F3

Paradox displays the Cust table. This was the first table you loaded to the desktop.

7. Switch back to the Customer table. To do this, press the Down Image key:

   F4

   Paradox redisplays the Customer table.

Section 14

Keys in the Table View

To move around in the table, use these key sequences:

Home	First record of the table
Up Arrow	Up one record
PgUp	Up one screen
Left Arrow	Left one field
Right Arrow	Right one field
Down Arrow	Down one record
PgDn	Down one screen
Ctrl-Home	First field of the table
Ctrl-End	Last field of the table
Ctrl-Left Arrow	Scroll left one full screen
Ctrl-Right Arrow	Scroll right one full screen

Section 15

Adding Information to a Table

Once the table has been created, you can add information to it. In this example, you add yourself to the Cust table just created.

1. First, make sure that the Cust table is displayed. Press the Up Image key:

    F3

    Paradox displays the empty table.

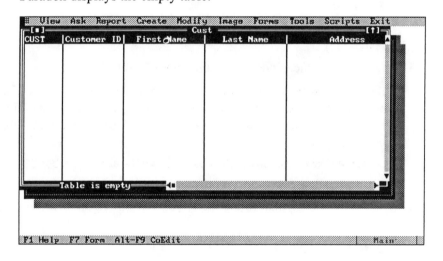

2. There are basically two ways to add records to the database: in Edit mode, or in DataEntry mode.

    First use the Edit mode. To do this, press:

    F9 [Edit]

Paradox moves the cursor down into the table and positions you in the first field for data entry. Note the mode indicator in the lower right corner of the status bar; it should read *Edit.*

3. From this position, type in a customer number of **1001**, then press **Enter**. The cursor moves to the First Name field. Continue entering your own name and address information until you reach the Zip Code field.

When you complete entry to the Zip Code field and press **Enter**, Paradox moves the cursor to the History field. Recall that this field is a memo field, designed to hold large bodies of text.

To add information to this field, you must enter the Field view mode. Enter the Field view mode by pressing either **Ctrl-F** or **Alt-F5**.

Press one of these key combinations now.

4. Paradox switches to its built-in text editor. Into the editor you may type as much text as you wish. Type:

This is one of our best customers. We have received several orders from this customer. Please make sure this customer receives the very best service.

When done, press:

F2 [DO-IT!]

5. Paradox closes the editor and returns to the Cust table.

Notice that you can see a portion of the History field. The amount of the History field visible is equal to the display length of the memo field. Whenever you want to look at the entire field, select the Field view command again.

Press **Enter**. Paradox moves the cursor down to record number 2.

If you wish, add a few more records to the table.

6. When done adding data to the table, you have three options. You can select:

[F2] DO-IT!   Saves your changes to the table.

[F10] Undo   Allows you to reverse changes to the table one step at a time.

[F10] Cancel   Cancels all changes to the table and leaves the Edit mode.

Select the command **DO-IT! [F2]** to save your changes. Paradox saves your changes to disk, then returns to the Main mode.

7. The second method for adding records to the table involves the DataEntry command. This method is better used when you want to add many records to the table at once, or if there are already a number of records present in the table.

   Select the commands:

   [F10] Menu/Modify/DataEntry

   Paradox displays a dialog box asking you which table to use. Press **Enter** to get a list of tables, then select the table **Cust**.

8. Paradox next displays a data entry table.

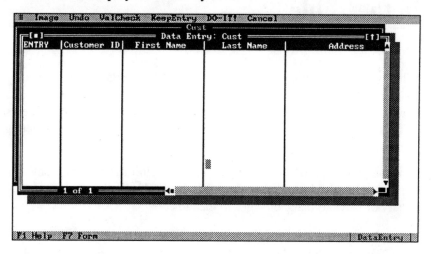

   Note that one of the differences between the Edit mode and the DataEntry mode is this: the DataEntry mode does not show any of the records already in the database.

   This is designed to prevent you from accidentally erasing the wrong records from the table.

   Type in a new record for customer 2001. Use any name and address information you want. When you come to the History field, enter the Field view mode (**Alt-F5** or **Ctrl-F**). Press **F2** to leave the Field view mode.

9. When finished entering records, press **F2** to save your changes and leave the DataEntry mode.

   Paradox returns to the desktop and displays the Cust table with the new records you just added.

Section 16

Editing Existing Information in the Table

While you are viewing your table, Paradox 4.5 prevents you from making any changes. This is done to guard against accidentally modifying parts of the table. However, you can tell Paradox 4.5 that you want to make changes to existing records in one of two ways: by pressing the Edit key [F9] or by selecting the commands F10/Modify/Edit.

Suppose you want to make changes to records in the Customer table. In this exercise you edit several records in the table. Along the way we will see a variety of ways to make changes to the table.

1. Display the Customer table by pressing the **F4 [Down Image]** key.

   Press the **Home** key to move to the first record. For the following examples, move the cursor to the Address field.

2. First change the Address field for this customer. Select the **Edit** command. To do this, press:

   F9 [Edit]

   To indicate that you are in the Edit mode, Paradox 4.5 displays the status indicator Edit in the lower right corner of the screen, as shown.

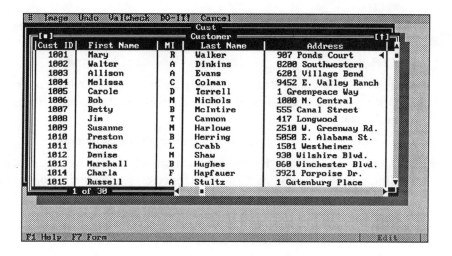

3. Now change this customer address. Use **Backspace** to erase all of the current address. Each press of Backspace erases one character at a time from a field.

   Type the new address:

   1961 Highland Street

   Press **Enter**.

   The cursor jumps to the City field. Press the **Left Arrow** key to move the cursor back to the Address field.

4. What if you want to edit the contents of a field by inserting characters *within* a field? To do this, it is best to use the Field view command.

   Next, edit the record for Walter Dinkins, containing the address 8200 Southwestern. Move to the Address field of this record.

   Select the command:

   Field view [Alt-F5]

   The cursor changes to a block. You can now edit the contents of the field without deleting existing parts of the entry.

5. Press the **Home** key to jump to the beginning of the field. Now type the new street number:

   945

   Press **Delete** several times to remove the old address number. Press the **Spacebar** to add a space after the new number. Press **Enter**.

The **Field view [Alt-F5]** command can also be executed by pressing these keys:

Ctrl-F

The Field view command is especially useful during the editing of a table. It lets you make changes within an existing entry without retyping the entire entry.

6. Two other key commands are useful during the edit process:

Ctrl-Backspace	The "Field Erase" command. During the edit process, pressing **Ctrl-Backspace** erases the entire contents of the current field.
Del	The "Delete Record" command. This command removes an entire record from the table. Be careful before executing this command.

7. When done editing this record, press **F2** to save your changes and return to the Main mode.

Section 17

Inserting New Records to the Table

There are three ways to enter new records to the table:

- While in the Edit mode, press **Insert**. Paradox 4.5 will open up a new record at the position of the cursor.
- While in the Edit mode and at the end of the table, press the **Down Arrow** key. Paradox will add a new record at the bottom of the table.
- When in the Main mode, press Main menu **[F10]/Modify/DataEntry**. This method allows you to enter several records at once.

You have already used the DataEntry method to add records to your table. In this exercise you reinforce the DataEntry method as well as use the remaining two methods to add records to Customer:

1. Move the cursor somewhere within the table, choosing any record you wish. Press **F9** to enter the Edit mode.

   Press the **Ins** key to insert a new recording to the table. Paradox 4.5 displays a blank record on the screen.

   Add yourself to the database. As you complete each field, press **Enter**.

2. Now add a record to the end of the table. To do this you must still be in the Edit mode.

   Press the **End** key to move to the end of the Customer table.

   Press the **Down Arrow** to add a new record to the end of the table. Add an acquaintance to the table.

   When done, press **F2** to save your changes.

3. The third way to add records to a table is to select the commands:

   Menu[F10]/Modify/DataEntry

Paradox asks you for a table name. Select the Customer table. Paradox displays an ENTRY table as shown below. A message at the top of the window tells you that this is a DataEntry table for the Customer table.

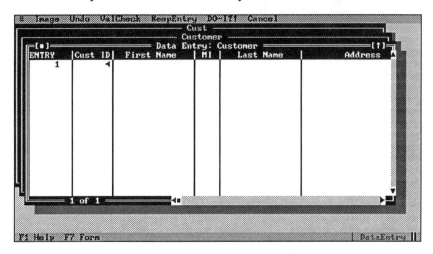

4. Records entered here are placed in a temporary table until you press the DO-IT! [F2] key. This way, if you accidentally edit or delete a record that should not have been modified, then only records in the temporary table can be harmed. The main table is protected from changes until you press the DO-IT! [F2] key.

Enter another record, then press the **DO-IT! [F2]** key. The new record is added to the Customer table, and Paradox returns to the Main mode.

Section 18

Undoing Changes

What if you make a mistake and wish to recover changes to a table? Paradox 4.5 provides an Undo facility that lets you reverse a series of changes to a table. It is important to note that this undo feature works only in the Edit mode.

To demonstrate the Undo facility, you will first make a couple of deletions to the Customer table.

1. First, place Paradox in the Edit mode. To do this, press the **Edit** key:

   F9

   Paradox 4.5 displays the Edit mode indicator in the lower right corner of the screen.

   Move to the end of the Customer table. To do this press the **End** key.

2. Delete this record. Press the **Del** key.

   The current record is deleted.

3. Now move to the beginning of the table by pressing the **Home** key.

4. Delete this record. Press the **Del** key.

   The first record of the table is deleted.

5. Now that you have made two deletions to the table, use the Undo facility of Paradox 4.5 to return these records to the table.

   Press **Undo [Ctrl-U]**

   The first record of the table is returned, as shown.

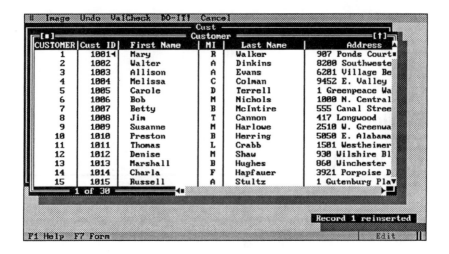

Press **Undo [Ctrl-U]** again. The second deleted record is returned to the table.

6. Use the Main menu to undo the next change to the table.

First, select the record for customer number 1006, Bob Nichols. Move to the First Name field. **Backspace** over the first name Bob and replace it with the name **Robert**.

7. Select the commands:

Edit menu [F10]/UnDo/Yes

Paradox restores the change to the first name entry in record 6.

The Undo feature allows you to restore all changes to a table that have been made in the current editing session. This means that once you press the DO-IT! [F2] command (discussed next), you cannot undo your changes anymore.

Section 19

Ending an Edit

When in the Edit mode, you can exit this mode in two ways:

   Select the **DO-IT!** command

   Select the **Cancel** command

The DO-IT! Command

The DO-IT! command tells Paradox 4.5 to post the changes you have just made to the table.

1. While in the Edit mode, if you press the F10 [Menu] key, the Edit menu is displayed. Notice the option: DO-IT!

2. Select the option: **DO-IT!** Paradox 4.5 saves all of your changes to this table.

   Paradox then returns to the Main mode.

NOTE   Be sure to select the Undo [Ctrl-U] command to recover any unintended changes *before* selecting the DO-IT! command.

   The function key F2 is also the DO-IT! key. Pressing this key during an Edit session tells Paradox 4.5 to save your changes thus far. Selecting the F2 function key is the same as executing the command:

   Menu [F10]/DO-IT!

The Edit Cancel Command

The Undo command is used to reverse changes to the table, one at a time. But what if you wanted to undo *all* of the changes made during an editing session? To do this use the Edit Cancel command.

1. To cancel all of the changes you have made during an edit session, select the commands:

   Menu [F10]/Cancel/Yes

   Paradox then returns to the Main mode. None of the changes you made to the table are saved.

Section 20

Sorting the Table

Normally the records in a Paradox table are displayed in the order in which they were entered. The exception to this comes when the table contains a key field. Key fields were discussed in the section called Creating a Paradox Table. When a key field exists, Paradox automatically sorts the table on the key field. Should it become necessary to change the normal order of a table, use the Modify Sort command. The Modify Sort command lets you sort the table on any field or any combination of fields, including memo fields.

If the table contains no key fields, Paradox asks you whether you want to sort into the same table, or into a new table. If you sort into the same table, the original order is lost. If you sort into a new table, the original table is preserved. If the table does contain a key field, Paradox will always sort into a new table in order to preserve the key in the original table.

In this exercise you sort the Customer table into new orders using several columns as sort keys.

1. After the last exercise the Customer table should still be on your screen. Notice that the table is currently sorted by the Customer ID field, as shown in the following illustration.

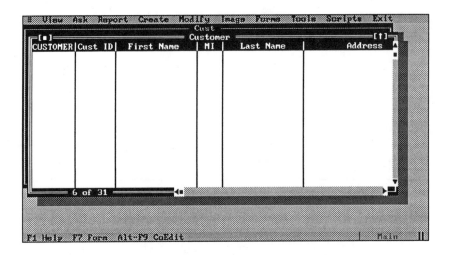

2. First, let us sort the table by the Last Name field. Select the commands:

   Menu [F10]/Modify/Sort

   Paradox asks you for a table name. Press **Enter**, then from the list select **Customer**.

3. Paradox asks if you want to sort to the same table, or to a new table name. Select the option:

   Same

   Paradox displays a sort form like the illustration below. Take a moment to read the sorting information at the top of this form.

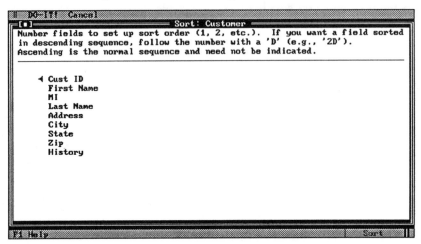

4. Tell Paradox to sort the table in ascending order by last name. Move the cursor to the Last Name field.

   Next to this field name, type the number **1**. Tell Paradox to carry out the sort. Press **DO-IT! [F2]**.

   Paradox will sort the table and redisplay Customer as shown below:

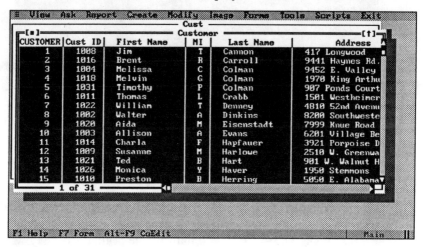

5. In the last sort, the table was sorted in ascending order on the Last Name field. Unless you tell Paradox otherwise, all sorts are completed in ascending order. However, it is easy to perform a descending sort.

   Sort the Customer table on Last Name again, this time in descending order.

   Select the commands:

   Menu [F10]/Modify/Sort

   Select the **Customer** table as before, then select the **Same** option.

6. Paradox shows you the sort form. Move the cursor to the Last Name field. Type:

   1D

   Press **Enter**. The number 1 tells Paradox to use this field as the primary sort key, and the letter D tells Paradox to sort in descending order.

7. Carry out the sort. Press:

   DO-IT! [F2]

   Paradox sorts the table and displays the results on the desktop:

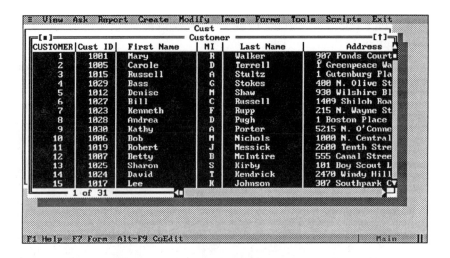

8. The first two sort operations used just one field. The next sort will work with multiple fields.

   Suppose you wanted to sort the customers by state, and within state by city. This sort requires a primary sort key (state) and a secondary sort key, (city). On the sort form you indicate the primary sort key with the number 1, and the secondary sort key with the number 2.

   Select the commands:

   Menu [F10]/Modify/Sort

   Select the **Customer** table as before, then select the **Same** option.

9. Paradox shows you the sort form. Move the cursor to the State field. Type:

   1

   Press **Enter**. Move to the City field. In this position, type:

   2

   Press **Enter**. Since you did not place the letter D after either entry, the sort will be carried out in ascending order. The sort will be carried out first on the State field. Whenever more than one record contains the same state entry, a secondary sort is performed on the City field.

10. Execute the sort. Press:

    DO-IT! [F2]

    Paradox sorts the table and displays the results. To see the City and State fields, press the right arrow key six times.

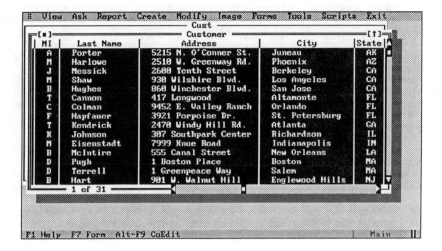

Examine the results of the sort. Note the arrangement of records for customers in California: the record for Berkeley comes first, the record for San Jose comes last.

11. Perform one last sort. This one will return the table to its original order. At the beginning of this exercise we noted that the table was in order by Cust ID.

    Sort in ascending order on this field to return this table to its original order.

    Select the commands:

    Menu [F10]/Modify/Sort

    Select the **Customer** table as before, then select the **Same** option.

12. Paradox shows you the sort form. Move the cursor to the Cust ID field. Type:

    1

    Carry out the sort. Press:

    DO-IT! [F2]

    Paradox sorts the table back to original order.

51

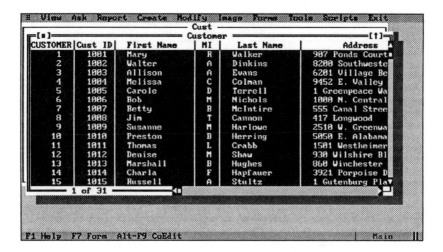

Section 21

Changing the Image Size of Tables

In the next few exercises you work with several commands: Clear Image, System Desktop, Image TableSize, Image ColumnSize, and Rotate [Ctrl-R]. These commands allow you to remove tables, and change the appearance of a table, or tables, on the screen.

In the next example, you modify the appearance of the desktop so that both the Customer table and the Transact table are visible at once. The Customer table was loaded in the previous section. The Transact table contains records of book orders from your customers, and it is loaded in this exercise.

Begin by loading the Transact table. Then, divide the screen in half, displaying parts of Customer and Transact. Next, change the column widths of fields in Customer. Finally, save these changes to Transact and Customer with the command Image KeepSet.

1. Begin by displaying the Main menu:

   Menu [F10]

   From the Main menu, select the option:

   View

   Press **Enter** to display a list of available tables. From the list choose Transact. Press **Enter**.

   Paradox 4.5 displays the Transact table:

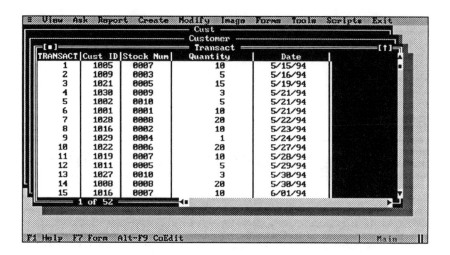

2. You now have a total of three tables in your desktop: Cust, Customer, and Transact. Only one of these tables is visible right now: Transact.

Note the appearance of the Transact table. Its border is a bright color compared to the other two tables. This means that Transact is the *active table*.

The active table is the table which your commands affect. Be sure to know which table is active whenever working with multiple tables.

In the following steps you divide the screen so that part of Customer and Transact are visible at the same time. This is a two-step process: First, remove the Cust table. Second, use the **System/Desktop/Tile** command to divide the desktop between the two remaining tables.

3. Remove the Cust table. To do this, press the **UpImage [F3]** key twice.

This step should make the Cust table the active table.

To remove the table, use the **ClearImage** key, **F8**. Press this key now.

Paradox removes the Cust table from the screen.

4. Next divide the desktop between the remaining two tables.

Press:

Alt-Spacebar

This key sequence activates the Paradox System menu, as shown below. This menu allows you to adjust the appearance of the desktop in a number of ways.

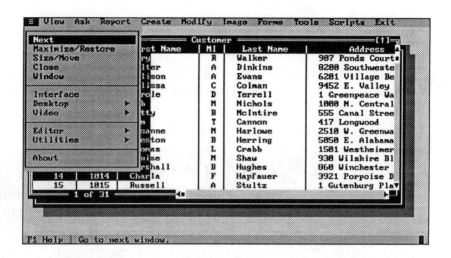

5. From the System menu, select the options:

Desktop/Tile

Paradox divides the desktop evenly between the Transact and Customer tables. Your screen should look like this illustration.

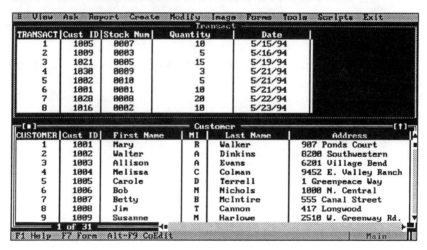

6. Another way to adjust the size of tables on the desktop involves the **Image TableSize** command.

First, press **UpImage [F3]** or **DownImage [F4]** to display the **Customer** table.

Next adjust the size for the Customer table.

55

7. Select the commands:

Main menu [F10]/Image/TableSize

Prompts at the top of the screen tell you to press the Up and Down Arrow keys to adjust the number of records visible.

Press the **Up Arrow** three times.

Press **Enter**. Your desktop should look like this.

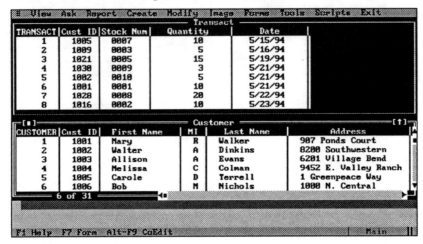

Using this technique, it is possible to display as many tables as screen space permits.

Section 22

Rotating Columns

The Rotate key [Ctrl-R] lets you change the way in which columns from a table are displayed. The Rotate command moves the column containing the cursor to the end of the table. Using this command, you can easily rearrange the appearance of any table.

To complete the example below, use the Customer table. If the table is not already loaded, select the View command and choose Customer. If the table is already loaded and is not visible, use the F3 [UpImage] or F4 [DownImage] command to display the Customer table.

Assume that you want to move the City field next to the Cust ID field in the Customer table.

1. First, change the display size of Customer back to full-screen size. This is not required but it will make the following illustrations more clear.

   Examine the Customer window on the screen. Notice the upper right corner of the window. In this location you should find the Maximize icon. The Maximize icon looks like this:

   [↑]

   Use the mouse to click on this icon.

2. Paradox resizes the Customer window to fill the entire desktop. If you do not have a mouse, you can maximize the Customer window by pressing:

   Alt-Spacebar [System menu]

   When the System menu is displayed, choose the option:

   Maximize/Restore

3. Press **Home** to move to the first record of the table. Next, use the **Right Arrow** to move the cursor to the First Name field (to the right of Cust ID).

   Press **Rotate**:

   [Ctrl-R]

   The MI (Middle Initial) field moves next to the Cust ID field. The First Name field moves to the last position in the table, at far right.

4. Press **Rotate** a second time:

   [Ctrl-R]

   The MI field moves to the end of the table. The Last Name field now appears next to the Cust ID field. Press **Rotate** a third time:

   [Ctrl-R]

   The Address field moves next to the Cust ID field. Press **Rotate** one final time. The City field is now next to the Cust ID field.

   Each time a column of the table is selected and the Rotate command is executed, the selected column will be moved to the far right in the table on screen. Using Rotate in this fashion it is possible for you to completely rearrange the appearance of the table.

5. If you wish to keep this arrangement of the table in the future, select the command:

   Menu [F10]/Image/KeepSet

   Paradox records the current arrangement of the table. The next time the table is loaded it will have the same appearance as the screen at the time you executed the KeepSet command.

Section 23

Locating Information in Columns

The Zoom command [Ctrl-Z] allows you to quickly locate a piece of information in the table.

Suppose you wanted to find a record for a customer named Carole Terrell. In general, to find a piece of information (such as the customer name "Carole Terrell") in the table using the Zoom command, follow these steps:

- Place the cursor in the field you wish to search, for example the Customer Name field.
- Press **[Ctrl-Z] Zoom**.
- Type **Carole Terrell** and press **Enter**.
- Paradox 4.5 moves to the first record containing "Carole Terrell."
- To find the next "Carole Terrell" record, press **[Alt-Z] Zoom Next**.
- Paradox 4.5 moves to the next "Carole Terrell" record, if any.

It is important to note that the cursor must be placed in the right field *before* you begin the Zoom command.

To complete the example below, use the Customer table. If the table is not already loaded, select the View command and choose Customer. If the table is already loaded and is not visible, use the F3 [UpImage] or F4 [DownImage] command to display the Customer table.

Suppose you want to find all the customers in the city of Dallas. Use the Zoom command to search for this information:

1. Use the **Left Arrow** or the **Right Arrow** to move the cursor to the City field.
2. Press:

   Zoom [Ctrl-Z].

3. A message is displayed in the status bar at the bottom of the screen:

Enter value (exact match or pattern) to search for.

Into the dialog box, type **Dallas,** and press **Enter.** (*Note:* This entry is case-sensitive and it must be typed as shown.)

4. The cursor moves to the first record in the table containing the city Dallas, as shown below.

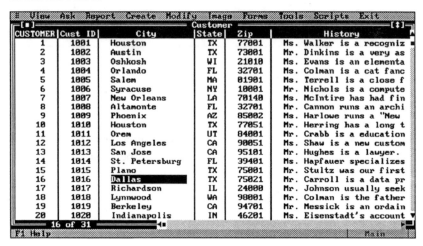

To find additional examples of customers in Dallas, press:

[Alt-Z] Zoom Next

The cursor jumps to the next record for a customer in Dallas.

The Zoom Next command moves the cursor to each new occurrence. When there are no more occurrences of a search value, Paradox displays the message "Match not found."

Section 24

Using Wild Card Characters to Locate Information

Wild card characters are used to provide general descriptions of something you wish to find in the table. For example, the string Sa.. would find Salem and San Francisco, but not St. Petersburg. The periods are the wild card characters. They tell Paradox 4.5 to find any entry that begins with Sa, no matter how many characters follow these two letters.

A second type of wild card involves the @ symbol. This wild card is a *place holder*. For example, the string Sa@@@ tells Paradox 4.5 to find an entry that begins with Sa and is followed by just three more characters. It would find Salem but not San Francisco.

In the exercise below, the .. and @ wild cards are used to search alphanumeric fields.

Make sure the Customer table is still in the desktop and the cursor is in the City field. Press the **Home** key to move to the first record.

1. Use the **..** wild card to create a search string for cities that begin with the letters **Sa**.

   Select the command:

   Zoom [Ctrl-Z].

2. A message is displayed in the status bar at the bottom of the screen:

   Enter value (exact match or pattern) to search for.

   Into the dialog box, type **Sa..** and press **Enter**. (*Note*: Entries using wild cards are *not* case sensitive.)

3. Paradox searches the City field and displays a record for Salem, as shown. Press the **Zoom Next** command:

    [Alt-Z]

    Paradox 4.5 searches for the next occurrence of a record that begins with **Sa,** and selects a record for San Jose.

```
# View Ask Report Create Modify Image Forms Tools Scripts Exit
┌─[■]──────────────────────────── Customer ───────────────────────[↕]─┐
│CUSTOMER│Cust ID│     City     │State│ Zip │        History         │
│   1    │ 1001  │Houston       │ TX  │77001│Ms. Walker is a recogniz ■
│   2    │ 1002  │Austin        │ TX  │73001│Mr. Dinkins is a very as
│   3    │ 1003  │Oshkosh       │ WI  │21010│Ms. Evans is an elementa
│   4    │ 1004  │Orlando       │ FL  │32701│Ms. Colman is a cat fanc
│   5    │ 1005  │███████████   │ MA  │01901│Ms. Terrell is a close f
│   6    │ 1006  │Syracuse      │ NY  │10001│Mr. Nichols is a compute
│   7    │ 1007  │New Orleans   │ LA  │70140│Ms. McIntire has had fin
│   8    │ 1008  │Altamonte     │ FL  │32701│Mr. Cannon runs an archi
│   9    │ 1009  │Phoenix       │ AZ  │85002│Ms. Harlowe runs a "New
│  10    │ 1010  │Houston       │ TX  │77051│Mr. Herring has a long t
│  11    │ 1011  │Orem          │ UT  │84001│Mr. Crabb is a education
│  12    │ 1012  │Los Angeles   │ CA  │90051│Ms. Shaw is a new custom
│  13    │ 1013  │San Jose      │ CA  │95101│Mr. Hughes is a lawyer.
│  14    │ 1014  │St. Petersburg│ FL  │39401│Ms. Hapfauer specializes
│  15    │ 1015  │Plano         │ TX  │75001│Mr. Stultz was our first
│  16    │ 1016  │Dallas        │ TX  │75021│Mr. Carroll is a data pr
│  17    │ 1017  │Richardson    │ IL  │24000│Mr. Johnson usually seek
│  18    │ 1018  │Lynnwood      │ WA  │98001│Mr. Colman is the father
│  19    │ 1019  │Berkeley      │ CA  │94701│Mr. Messick is an ordain
│  20    │ 1020  │Indianapolis  │ IN  │46201│Ms. Eisenstadt's account ▼
╞════════ 5 of 31 ════════════════◄■════════════════════════════►■═╡
│F1 Help                                                      Main  │
```

4. Continue pressing **[Alt-Z]** to find any additional records that match the search value. When Paradox finds no more matches for the value entered, it displays the message:

    Match not found

5. The Paradox wild card characters can also be used to enclose an expression. Now move to the First Name field. Select the command:

    Zoom [Ctrl-Z]

    Type the expression:

    ..ar..

    Press **Enter**. Paradox moves to a record containing **Mary** in the First Name field. Notice that this arrangement of wild cards, in front of and behind the letters "ar" tells Paradox to find the characters "ar" anywhere in the field.

6. Press **Zoom Next [Alt-Z]** to move to the next matching record. Paradox 4.5 will find records for **Marshall, Charla,** and **Carole** because all of these names contain the string "ar" embedded in the name.

    Press **Zoom Next [Alt-Z]** one more time.

Now Paradox jumps to a record for **Sharon**. The search value **..ar..** will locate any first name containing the letters "ar."

7. A second kind of wild card in Paradox, the @ sign, is used as a place holder. For example, suppose you wanted to find first names that begin with a "B" and are followed by just three more letters.

   To do this, select the command:

   Zoom [Ctrl-Z]

   Backspace over the previous entry, then type the expression:

   B@@@

   Press **Enter**.

8. Paradox moves to the record for **Bill**.

   Pressing the **Zoom Next [Alt-Z]** command locates a record for **Bass**.

   Pressing the **Zoom Next [Alt-Z]** command one more time displays the "Match not found" message, because no other first names meet this condition.

Section 25

Removing Tables from the Desktop

Occasionally the desktop can become crowded with too many tables. To remove a table from the desktop, use the Clear Image command. There are two versions of this command. The first, ClearImage [F8], removes the current table from the desktop. The second, ClearAll [Alt-F8], removes all tables from the desktop.

1. From earlier exercises, you should have the Customer and the Transact tables in the desktop already. You can verify this by selecting the **UpImage [F3]** or the **DownImage [F4]** commands.

   If either of these tables is not present, use the following commands to bring them to the desktop:

   Main menu [F10]/View

2. Now add a third table to the desktop. Select the commands:

   Main menu [F10]/View

   From the list of tables, select **Inven**. The Inven table appears on the desktop as shown:

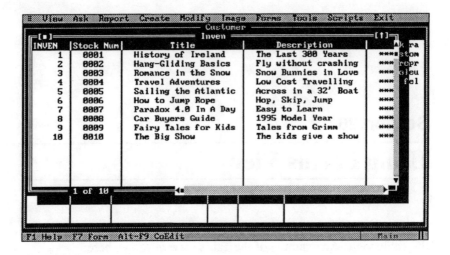

3. Now remove the Inven table by selecting the command:

   Clear Image [F8]

   Paradox Removes the Inven table from the desktop, leaving the Customer and Transact tables.

4. Now remove the remaining tables with one command, Clear All. Select the command:

   Clear All [Alt-F8]

   Paradox removes all the tables from the desktop and redisplays the Main menu.

Section 26

Using Forms View

In previous exercises Paradox 4.5 displayed the records in your tables using the Table view. An example of the Table view is shown here:

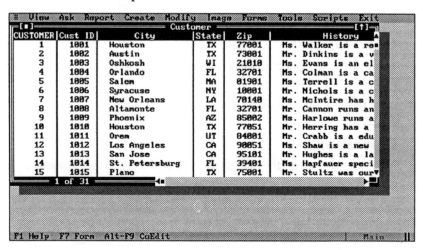

The Table view shows a list of many records on the screen at once. Notice that although you can see many records at once, frequently you cannot see *all* of any one record.

Paradox also allows you to look at a single record at a time. This is done using the Forms view. The Forms view differs from the Table view in this respect: The Forms view shows you all the information about a single record in the table. More complex forms can show all the information about a single entity, even though this information is located in more than one table.

Paradox can maintain as many as fifteen forms for each table. These forms can be custom-designed, or Paradox can create a standard form.

In the following exercises you use the Customer table along with the Transact table to view information using different forms.

Before you begin these examples, bring these two tables to the desktop:

1. Press **F10 [Main menu]** to activate the Main menu, then select the **View** option.

   When Paradox asks you to type a table name, press **Enter**.

2. Select **Customer** from the list. Press **Enter**.

3. Repeat this process to load the Transact table to the desktop.

   Press **F10 [Main menu]** to activate the Main menu, then select the **View** option.

   When Paradox asks you to type a table name, press **Enter**. Now select **Transact** from the list of tables displayed.

   Because the Transact table was loaded last, it should be the table currently displayed. If it is not, use the **F3 [Up Image]** or the **F4 [Down Image]** keys to display the Transact table.

   Now that you have loaded the Customer and Transact tables, proceed to the next series of exercises. In these exercises you modify the appearance of the desktop to display the Forms view.

Section 27

A Standard Form

Every time you create a new table structure, Paradox also creates a standard Paradox form. The standard form includes all the fields in the table. The name of the table and the current record number are displayed at the top of the form window.

1. Make sure the Transact table is the active window. If it is not, use the **Up Image [F3]** or the **Down Image [F4]** keys to display Transact.

2. Press the **Forms Toggle [F7]** key. Paradox displays an automatically created standard form on the desktop, as shown below.

   The standard form displays all of the fields in the Transact table.

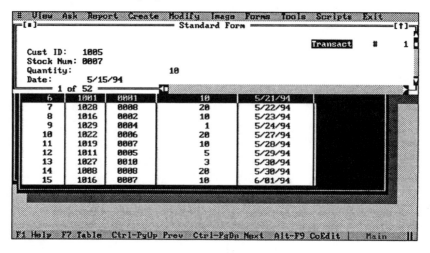

Because F7 is a toggle key, you can easily switch between the Table and Forms views.

Pressing F7 from the Forms view redisplays the Table view. Pressing F7 again switches you back to the Forms view. Note that Paradox keeps the cursor in the same field in both views.

3. Press the **F7** key a few times to demonstrate this. End up on the Forms view.

4. With the **Forms view** on the screen, move the cursor from field to field. Notice that movement in the Forms view is similar to that in the Table view. In fact, the navigation keys in the Forms view are the same as the navigation keys in the Table view.

   Try using the arrow keys to move up and down in the table. Be sure to note the way the **Home** and **End** keys move to the top and bottom of the table. To edit a field in a record, press the **Edit** key **[F9]** to enter the Edit mode.

5. Try using several of the key commands below to move around in the Forms view:

Home	Move to the first record of the table
Up Arrow	Move the cursor up one field
PgUp	Move the cursor up one record
Left Arrow	Move the cursor left in the current field
Right Arrow	Move the cursor right in the current field
Down Arrow	Move the cursor down one field
PgDn	Move the cursor down one record
Ctrl-Home	Move the cursor to the first field of the table
Ctrl-End	Move the cursor to the last field of the table

Section 28

A Simple Custom Form

If the standard form that Paradox automatically creates is not satisfactory, then you can create a custom form for that table. In this example, you create a simple custom form for the Transact table.

When completed, your customized form will look like this illustration:

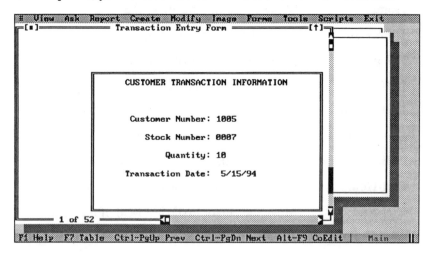

For this example, make sure the Transact table is currently displayed. It does not matter whether the Table view or the Forms view is now displayed.

1. Create a custom form for Transact. Select the commands:

   Main menu [F10]/Forms/Design

   When Paradox asks for the name of a table, select the **Transact** table. Press **Enter**.

2. Paradox displays a list of forms. The first, indicated by the letter F, represents the Standard Form, as seen in the previous section.

   Notice the description for the form displayed on the right of the dialog box.

3. Move the cursor to form number **1**. Notice the description:

   Unused form

   Press **Enter**.

4. Paradox asks for a Form description: Type the following description:

   Transaction Entry Form

   Press **Enter**.

   Now Paradox displays a forms design screen.

   Notice the cursor position is displayed in the lower left corner of the forms design screen. It is shown as **1, 1**. The indication **1:1** represents page 1 of 1. Move the cursor to position **5, 15**.

5. Paradox uses a specialized menu when in the forms design mode. Activate this menu by pressing:

   Forms menu [F10]

   The Forms menu provides commands to help you design and save a custom form. Use this menu to place a border around the center portion of the screen. Select the commands:

   Border/Place/Double-Line

6. Paradox displays a message at the top of the screen telling you to use the arrow keys to position the cursor at one corner of the screen.

   The cursor is at position **5, 15**. This is the upper left corner of the box. To anchor the cursor at this position, press **Enter**.

7. Paradox now tells you to move to the diagonal corner. Press **Down Arrow** fifteen times.

   Now press **Right Arrow** key forty-five times. This creates a box-shaped area on your screen.

   Press **Enter**. Your screen looks like the following illustration:

71

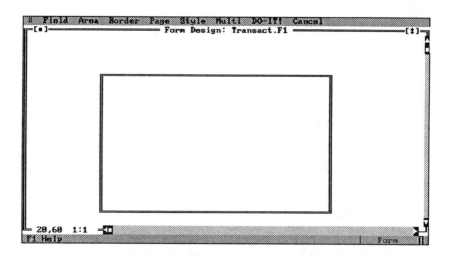

8. Next, enter the text within the box.

Move the cursor to position **6, 22**. Type a title for the custom form:

CUSTOMER TRANSACTION INFORMATION

Press **Enter**.

9. Now enter labels for the field names in the form. Move to the position **10, 23**. Type the field label:

Customer Number:

Press **Enter**. Now place three more labels below this first one, each at the positions shown below.

Field Label	*Position*
Stock Number:	**12, 26**
Quantity:	**14, 30**
Transaction Date:	**16, 22**

When the field labels are entered, your form looks like this:

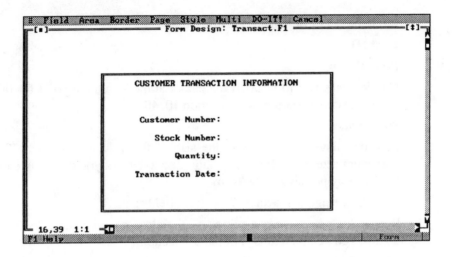

10. So far, all entries made to your form have been descriptive text. Now add the data fields from the Transact table to your form.

    Position the cursor at 10, 40. Select the commands:

    Menu [F10]/Field/Place

    Paradox can place several kinds of fields on the screen. This time select the **Regular** field type.

    Paradox 4.5 displays a list of field names, as seen here:

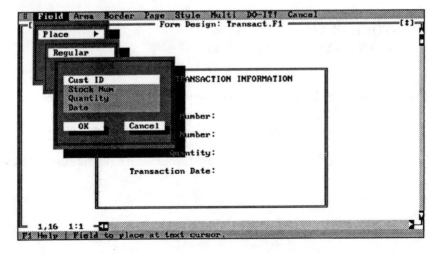

11. From the list of field names displayed, select:

    Cust ID

    Press **Enter**.

    Paradox asks you to position the cursor at the beginning point for this field. The cursor should be at position 10, 40.

    Press **Enter**.

    Paradox allows you to adjust the size of the field on the form. The maximum size of the field is initially displayed, but you can reduce the field size by pressing **Left Arrow**.

    Press **Enter** again to accept the current field size.

12. Repeat this process to place three more fields on your custom form. To do this, you complete this command selection:

    Menu [F10]/Field/Place/Regular

    Before selecting these commands, remember to position the cursor at the starting position of the field.

    Next, select the command above. Paradox 4.5 asks you to position the cursor at the beginning point for each field. Press **Enter**.

    Finally, adjust the field size if necessary using the **Left Arrow**, and press **Enter** a second time.

13. Place the data fields in the following positions:

Field Name	*Position*
STOCK NUM:	**12, 40**
QUANTITY:	**14, 40**
DATE:	**16, 40**

NOTE When the QUANTITY field has been selected, it will extend beyond the border of your box. Simply press the **Left Arrow** to trim the field length. Trim it until it is six positions long.

When the field labels are been entered, your form looks like the following illustration.

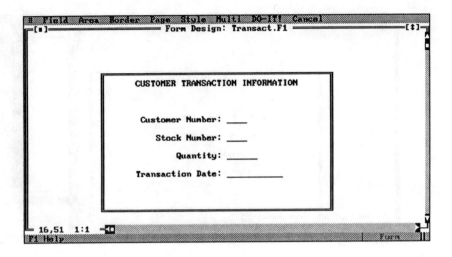

14. The custom form is complete. Tell Paradox to create and save the form you have designed. Press the key:

DO-IT! [F2]

Paradox creates and saves your custom form, then returns to the Main mode.

15. Notice that the form is not automatically displayed. Tell Paradox to display the form with the commands:

Menu [F10]/Image/Pickform

From the list of defined forms, select number **1**, the one with the "Transaction Entry Form" description.

When you select the first form, Paradox displays a record from the Transact table, as shown here.

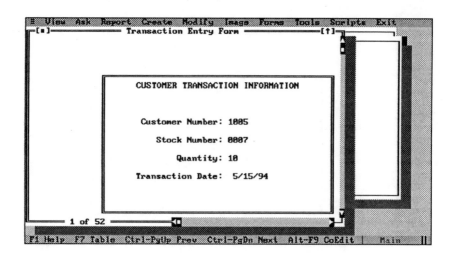

Navigation and editing on this form follow the same rules for editing in the Table view, discussed earlier.

Enhancing the Custom Form

In the last exercise you created a simple custom form for the Transact table. This custom form displayed all the fields of the table.

The addition of validity checks is one of the most important steps you can take to ensure that correct information gets into your table. To create validity checks, you define the highest and lowest allowable values for a field. If an entry falls outside these limits, Paradox displays an error message. In this exercise you enhance this basic form with validity checks.

1. If the Transact form is not displayed, bring it to the screen. To do this, select the commands:

   Menu [F10]/Image/Pickform

   From the list of defined forms, select number **1**, the one with the "Transaction Entry Form" description.

   When you select the first form, Paradox displays a record from the Transact table as shown below.

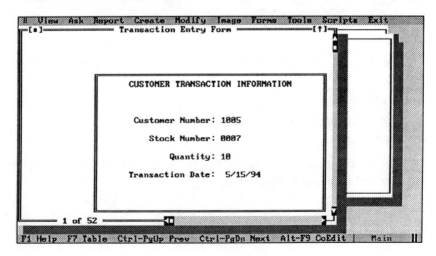

2. Now begin modifying the form. You will add validity checks to the form. These will perform tests on data to make sure it falls within limits you establish.

   To create validity checks in Paradox 4.5 you must be in the Edit mode. Select the commands:

   Menu [F10]/Modify/Edit

   Paradox 4.5 asks you to choose a table. Select the Transact table. Paradox displays the screen in Edit mode.

   Remember: You can also go to the Edit mode by pressing the **Edit [F9]** key.

3. Activate the Edit menu by pressing:

   Menu [F10]

   Paradox activates the Edit menu as shown in this illustration:

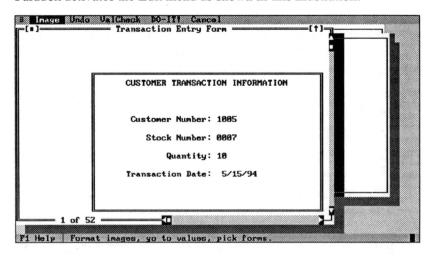

4. Notice the option called ValCheck. This option lets you define or remove tests carried out during data entry. Select the option:

   ValCheck

   You will *define* new values. Select the option:

   Define

5. Paradox displays a message asking you to move to the correct field. Move to the Customer Number field.

   Press **Enter**.

   Paradox displays a new menu, one that shows all your ValCheck options:

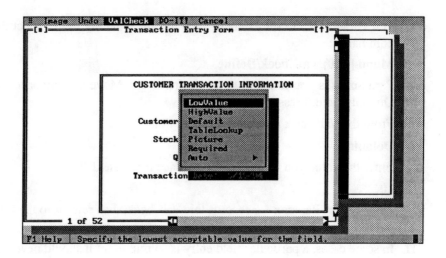

6. Suppose you wanted to establish a limit on the range of customer numbers. The lowest customer number should be 1000, and the highest customer number should be 2000.

   Select the option:

   LowValue

   Paradox asks you to enter the lowest allowable value for this field. Type **1000**. Press **Enter**.

   Paradox 4.5 records this ValCheck, then returns to the Edit mode.

7. Set the highest value for the field. Select the commands:

   Menu [F10]/ValCheck/Define

   Paradox asks you to move to the desired field. Leave the cursor in the Customer Number field. Press **Enter**.

8. From the ValCheck menu, select the option:

   HighValue

   Type the highest acceptable value: **2000**. Press **Enter**. Once again, Paradox 4.5 records this ValCheck, then returns to the Edit mode.

9. In many cases, a default entry can be helpful. For example, suppose your standard order quantity is 10 copies of a book. Using the ValCheck options, Paradox can place this value in the field for you.

Tell Paradox 4.5 to set a default value for the Quantity field. Select the commands:

Menu [F10]/ValCheck/Define

Paradox asks you to move to the desired field. Move the cursor to the Quantity field. Press **Enter**.

10. From the ValCheck menu, select the option:

Default

Enter the value you want Paradox to place in the field. Type:

10

Press **Enter**. Paradox 4.5 records this ValCheck, then returns to the Edit mode.

11. In some cases, a particular field entry is so important it should never be left blank. Assume that the Date field is such a field. Using the ValCheck options, you can make this field a Required field.

Select the commands:

Menu [F10]/ValCheck/Define

Paradox asks you to move to the desired field. Move the cursor to the Date field. Press **Enter**.

12. From the ValCheck menu, select the option:

Required

Paradox displays a menu asking you to confirm that this field is a required field. Select the option:

Yes

Press **Enter**. Paradox 4.5 records this ValCheck, then returns to the Edit mode.

13. Now, add a record to the end of the Transact table to see the ValCheck settings in action.

To move to the end of the table press the **End** key. Now press **Down Arrow** to display a blank record, as shown here.

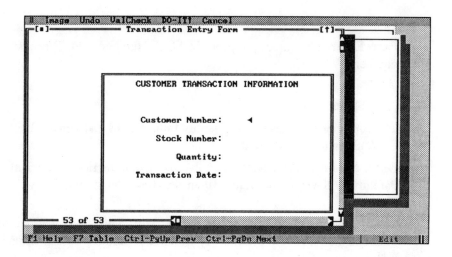

14. Enter a customer number outside the high and low values you established. Type a low value:

900

Press **Enter**. Paradox 4.5 displays a message showing the expected values.

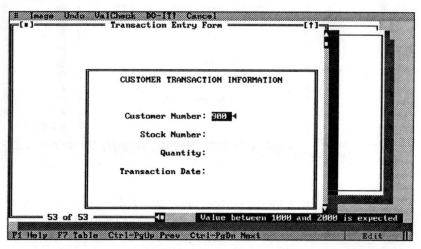

Paradox would display a similar message if your entry exceeded the highest allowable value for this field.

15. Press the **Backspace** key three times to erase the old value. Type a new value:

1053

Press **Enter**. The cursor jumps to the Stock Number field. Type a stock number:

0007

Press **Enter**.

16. The cursor next jumps to the Quantity field. Recall that you established a default value for this field.

    Leave this field blank. Instead, let Paradox fill in the field. Press **Enter**. Paradox will place the value **10** in the field, as shown in the next illustration.

17. Finally, the cursor moves to the Date field. This field was earlier designated as a required field. Try to leave it blank. To do this, press **Enter**.

    Paradox displays a new message, as shown in the illustration.

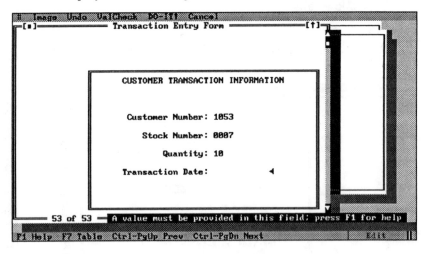

18. Fill in the field with the current date, then press **Enter**. Now save the record and leave the Edit mode. Press the **[F2] DO-IT!** key.

Section 30

A Multi-record Form

In addition to a single record, Paradox can also display a custom form showing more than one record in a single table. In this example, you create a custom form for Transact to display a set of five records at a time. When done, your custom form will look like this:

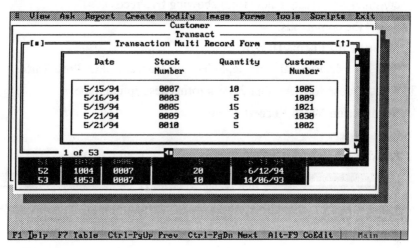

1. The custom form from Transact should still be on the screen. If it is not, select the commands:

   Menu [F10]/Image/Pickform

   From the list of defined forms, select number **1**, the one with the "Transaction Entry Form" description. When you have selected this form, Paradox displays a record from the Transact table.

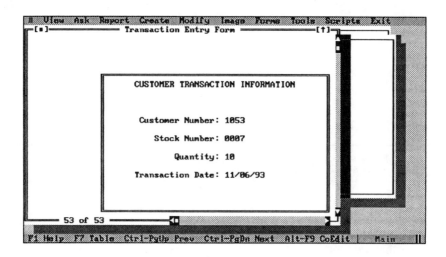

2. Note that this form shows just one record at a time. Use the Forms Design commands to create a new form showing five records.

Select the commands:

Menu [F10]/Forms/Design

Paradox asks for a table name. Select the Transact table. Press **Enter**.

3. Next, choose form number **2**. As a forms description, type:

Transaction Multi Record Form

Press **Enter**.

Paradox 4.5 now displays the forms design screen:

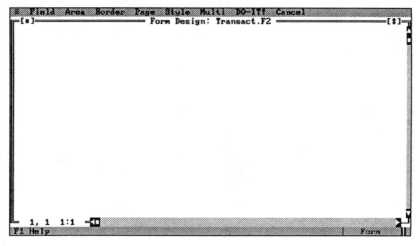

4. First, position the column headers for each field. Recall that the cursor position is displayed in the lower left corner of the screen. In the illustration it is displayed as **1, 1**. Use the following table to enter the text.

Field Label	*Position*
Date	**2, 15**
Stock	**2, 27**
Number	**3, 27**
Quantity	**2, 40**
Customer	**2, 53**
Number	**3, 54**

When the field labels are entered, your form looks like this:

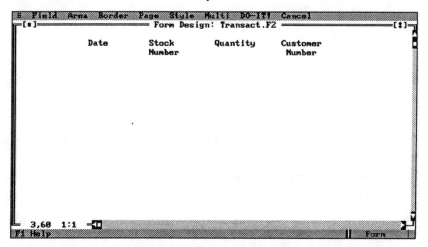

5. Now place the data fields on your form. To do this, you use the command:

Menu [F10]/Field/Place/Regular

When Paradox 4.5 displays a list of field names, select each field and position it using the table below. Note that you will have to trim the length of the Quantity field. Make it 8 positions in length, starting under the "Q" in the header Quantity and ending under the "y" in Quantity.

Field Name	*Position*
DATE	**5, 12**
STOCK NUMBER	**5, 28**
QUANTITY	**5, 40**
CUST ID	**5, 55**

When the data fields are positioned, your form looks like this:

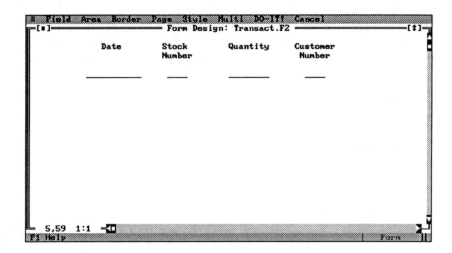

6. Save your work to this point. Press the **DO-IT!** key:

   F2

   Paradox saves the form.

7. With a row of fields defined on the form, you can now tell Paradox 4.5 to repeat these fields four more times. In the following steps you create a scrolling region on your custom form. Select the commands:

   Menu [F10]/Forms/Change

   As the table name, select **Transact**.

8. Paradox asks you which form should be changed. Select form number **2**.

   Paradox asks if you want to change the description for the form. Leave it unchanged. Press **Enter**.

   Paradox displays the forms design screen, as seen here:

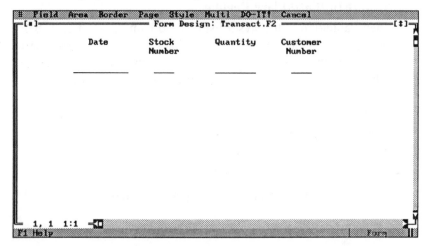

9. Now tell Paradox that you want to see multiple records on the form. Select the commands:

   Menu [F10]/Multi/Records/Define

   Paradox asks you to move the cursor to the corner of the region to define. Move the cursor to the first position of the DATE field, at location **5, 12**. Press **Enter**.

10. The next message instructs you to move to the diagonal corner of the region.

    Press **Right Arrow** until you reach the end of the CUST NUMBER field, at location **5, 58**. Your screen should look like this:

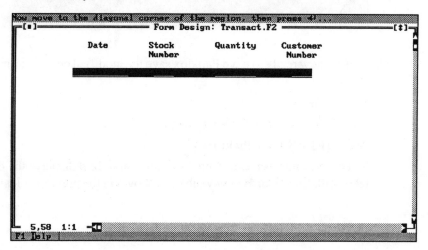

11. Press **Enter** to complete your selection. Paradox tells you to press the **Down Arrow** or **Up Arrow** keys to add or delete rows to or from the region.

    Press **Down Arrow** four times, then press **Enter** to complete the selection.

12. As a last step, place borders around parts of your new form. To do this, use the commands:

    Menu [F10]/Border/Place

    Select either **Single** or **Double**, then follow the messages on the screen. They will ask you move the cursor to opposite corners of the box you are defining.

    Use the following illustration to position the boxes.

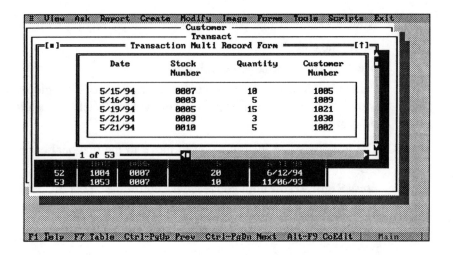

13. You are now ready to have Paradox save the modified custom form. Press the key:

DO-IT! [F2]

To display the new table, select the commands:

Menu [F10]/Image/Pickform

Select form number **2**, and press **Enter**. Paradox redisplays the custom table with five records now visible, as shown in the previous illustration.

Section 31

Asking Questions of a Paradox Table

Paradox uses what is called the Query By Example, or QBE, technique for asking questions about information in a Paradox table.

This method is called Query By Example because you fill out a Query Form to create an example of the information you are looking for. A Query Form looks like a Paradox table without any data in it. By moving to a particular field in the query form and pressing the Checkmark [F6] key, that field is selected for display in the Answer Table. The Answer Table is a subset of the current table that contains information matching your Query By Example.

In this example, you want to ask questions about orders in the Transact table.

1. The Transact table should already be in the desktop.

    Press the **Up Image [F3]** or **Down Image [F4]** keys to display the Transact table. Then press the **Form Toggle [F7]** key to display the Table view in the desktop.

    Your screen should look like the following illustration.

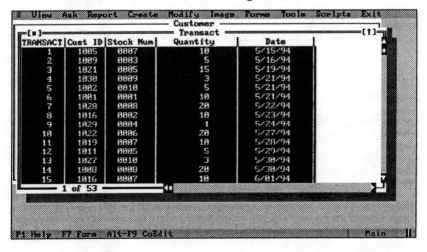

2. Notice the Stock Num column in the table. It contains the stock number of each book ordered by various customers.

   Suppose you wanted to know how many copies of stock number 0005 have been sold, to which customers, and on which dates.

3. Select the commands:

   Menu [F10]/Ask

   When Paradox requests a table name, select the **Transact** table. Paradox displays a blank query form from this table, as shown below.

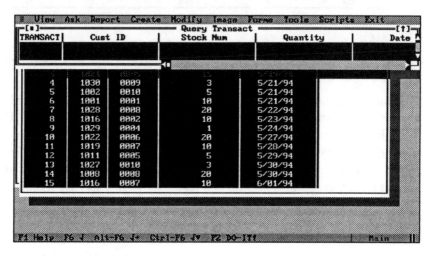

The query form contains all of the fields from Transact. Now tell Paradox which fields to display.

4. Move the cursor to the Cust ID field and press the key:

   Checkmark [F6]

   Notice the small checkmark symbol that appears in the Cust ID field.

   Select the remaining fields for this query. Move to the Stock Num field and enter:

   0005

   After making this entry, press the **Checkmark [F6]** key to place a check in the Stock Number field.

5. Move to the Quantity field. Place a check in this field. Finally, highlight the Date field and press the key:

   Checkmark [F6]

Once again a small checkmark symbol appears in the field. You have selected all the fields in the table. By placing the entry "0005" in the Stock Number field, you instruct Paradox to look only for records containing this entry in the field.

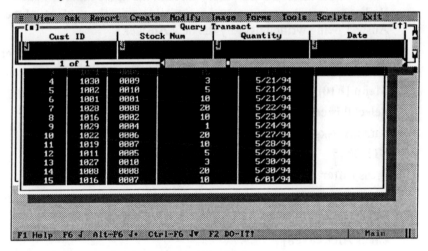

6. Tell Paradox to carry out the query. To do this, press:

DO-IT! [F2]

Paradox searches the Transact table and displays an Answer table, as shown here.

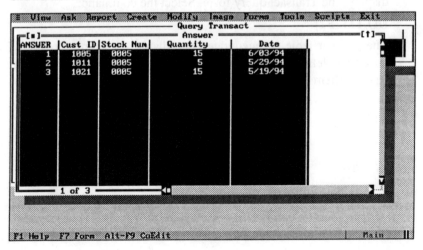

7. This Answer table can be manipulated just like any other Paradox table: Browse it, edit it, or display a standard form for it by pressing **Form Toggle [F7]**.

   The Answer table is a temporary table in the sense that the next Query By Example will create a new Answer table, with the contents of the old Answer being written over by the new Answer.

8. A useful feature of Paradox is its ability to save this query and repeat it again at a later time. This is done with the command:

   Menu [F10]/Scripts/QuerySave

   Select this command now.

   Paradox asks you enter a query script name. Type:

   STK0005

   Press **Enter**.

9. Now run your query a second time using the script you just recorded.

   First, clear the desktop by selecting the command:

   Clear All [Alt-F8]

   Next, select the commands:

   Menu [F10]/Scripts/Play

   Select the script name **STK0005** and press **Enter**.

10. Paradox again executes the commands used to create the query, then displays the Transact query form. Select the command:

    DO-IT! [F2]

    The Answer table is regenerated and displayed. Using the QuerySave command lets you create complex queries just once, then save and execute them again later.

    Such queries can also be included in the PAL programming language in Paradox.

Section 32

Using QBE to Calculate Statistics

In a query form the CALC SUM operator can be used to produce a summary of a field. For example, in the last query you displayed the number of copies of stock number 0005 sold by customer number. What if you wanted to know the total number of this volume that have been sold? To do this you will modify the first query form.

After the last exercise, the Answer table was displayed. Next, move back to the query form and modify it:

1. Select the command **Up Image [F3]** until the Transact query form is displayed.

   Now modify the query form so that it calculates the sum of stock number 0005 that have been ordered.

2. Move to the Cust ID field.

   Press the **Checkmark [F6]** key. Because this field previously had a checkmark in it, pressing this key a second time removes the checkmark.

3. Leave the Stock Num field alone. Instead, move the cursor right to the Quantity field.

   Press the **Checkmark [F6]** key. As with the Cust ID field, this field had a checkmark in it, and pressing this key a second time removes the checkmark.

   In place of the checkmark, type **CALC SUM** in the Quantity field and press **Enter**.

4. Finally, move to the Date field. Remove the check present here by pressing the **Checkmark [F6]** key. Your query should look like this:

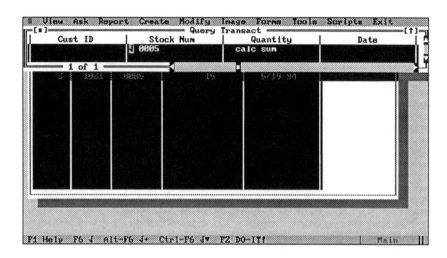

Your query now asks Paradox to calculate the sum of stock number 0005 that have been ordered.

5. Tell Paradox to execute the query by pressing the **DO-IT!** [F2] key.

   This time the Answer table contains only one record: the total number of this volume ordered. An example of the Answer table is shown in the following illustration.

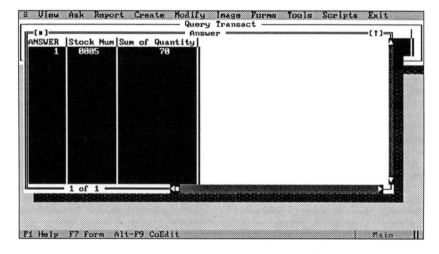

6. There are additional calculations which can be carried out using the CALC operator. These include:

CALC AVERAGE   Calculates an average in a numeric field

CALC MIN   Calculates the minimum value in a numeric field

CALC MAX   Calculates the maximum value in a numeric field

7. Move the cursor to the Quantity field, then try each of the above expressions. Remember to press the **DO-IT!** key after you have entered each expression, then compare results.

As you carry out each query, Paradox 4.5 creates a new Answer table to replace the one created for the previous query.

Section 33

Reports in Paradox 4.5

Paradox 4.5 comes with a report generator that creates and prints either a standard report or as many as fifteen custom reports. In the coming exercises, you print examples of both standard and custom reports.

Paradox standard reports are created automatically for each table in Paradox. These standard reports can be printed quickly using the Instant Report [Alt-F7] command.

Paradox custom reports are reports that you design. These custom reports can be either *tabular reports* or *free-form* reports. Recall the appearance of the desktop when you are using the Table view: rows and columns of data. Now recall the appearance of the Forms view: fields positioned anywhere on the screen. As you will see, a tabular report looks like a table, and a free-form report looks like a form.

Let's begin with an example of an instant report. To produce an instant report you need only have a table on the desktop. An instant report will always be sent directly to the printer. All the fields and all the records in the table will be included in the report. Make sure your printer is ready to print before you select the Instant Report [Alt-F7] command.

Create an instant report on the Transact table by first clearing the desktop and loading Transact.

1. Select the command:

   Clear All [Alt-F8]

2. Load the Transact table with the commands:

   Menu [F10]/View

   From the list of tables, select the **Transact** table and press **Enter**.

3. Check your printer to make sure it is turned on and ready to go, then select the command:

Instant Report [Alt-F7]

A standard report is sent to the printer.

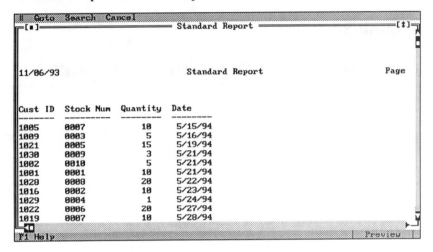

4. Examine the standard report. This report will consist of a date and page number on each page, as well as all the fields in the table. A standard report like this can be printed for *any* Paradox table. This means that you can easily produce a report from an Answer table. Recall that the Answer table is a temporary table created in answer to a query.

Pressing the Instant Report [Alt-F7] command after creating the Answer is one way to easily compare results of several queries. Paradox will send the entire contents of the Answer table to the printer.

Section 34

A Simple Custom Tabular Report

In the last exercise, you sent a standard report to the printer. This standard report consisted of all the fields and all the records in the Transact table. You might wish to rearrange the fields in the report or exclude some fields from the report. In such cases the standard report is not sufficient.

In this exercise you create and customize a report for the Customer table. Suppose you wanted to print a Customer Directory for the use of your employees. The content of such a report would typically contain "name-and-address" type information in a columnar format. This kind of report in Paradox 4.5 is called a Tabular report because it resembles the Table view with which you are familiar. Create this report next.

1. Bring the Customer table to the desktop.

   Select the commands:

   Menu [F10]/View

   Press **Enter** to see a list of tables and select the **Customer** table.

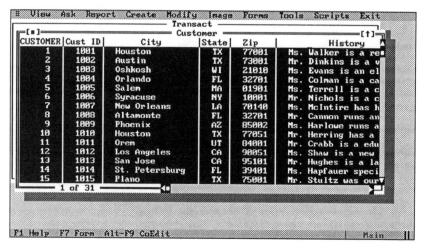

2. Notice that the table is wider than the desktop on your screen. This is a signal that your report width may need to be adjusted so that it can fit on a standard sheet of paper.

   Begin creating your report. Select the commands:

   Menu [F10]/Report

   Examine the various report options displayed on the menu. You will use the Design option first to create the report specifications. Select:

   Design

3. Paradox 4.5 asks you for a table name. Select the **Customer** table.

   Next you are asked to select a report number.

   Note that, as with forms, you can maintain as many as fifteen separate report forms for each table. The first report, designated **R**, is always the standard report.

   Select report number **1**, the first unused report.

4. Paradox now asks you for a report description.

   The description you enter here will appear in two places: in the reports menu as a report description, and as a page header on the printed report.

   Type in the description:

   Customer Directory

   Press **Enter**.

5. Next you are asked to choose a report type: Tabular or Free-Form. Choose the option:

   Tabular

   Paradox 4.5 now displays the tabular report design screen.

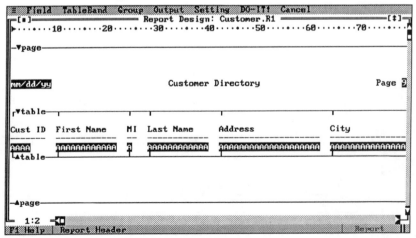

Notice the ruler line at the top of the screen. It tells you which column of the page the cursor rests in, and it helps you position fields in the report.

6. The desktop is divided into three sections: a Page Band at the top of the screen, the Table Band in the middle of the screen, and a Page Band at the bottom of the screen.

   The Page Bands at top and bottom of the screen can be thought of as page headers and footers. The contents of these bands will be printed at the top and bottom of each new page of the report.

   The Table Band at the center of the desktop reflects the body of the report. The Table Band will be printed once for each record sent to the printer.

   Move your cursor to the upper Page Band.

7. Examine this page band. It contains several blank rows. Starting at the left edge of the screen, it contains a date, then your report description as a title, and finally a page number at the right.

   Suppose you decide to reduce the number of blank rows in the header. To do this, position the cursor on a blank row in the header Page Band. Make sure the cursor rests at the *beginning* of the blank line.

   Now select the command:

   Report/Line/Delete [Ctrl-Y]

   Paradox 4.5 deletes a blank line from the upper Page Band. This leaves more room on the page for customer information.

8. Move the cursor to the lower Page Band, where we will add a footer. Near the bottom of the lower Page Band, place the phrase:

   Report prepared by: Your Name Here

   When these steps are completed, your report definition looks like this:

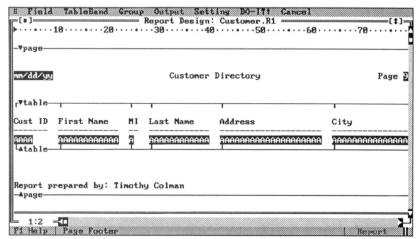

9. Now let's turn our attention to the Table Band. This is the heart of your report. Move the cursor to the Table Band.

   The Table Band extends beyond the right edge of the screen. To examine the fields beyond the right edge of the screen, select the command:

   [Ctrl-End]

   The cursor jumps to the far right edge of the report specification. As you can see, you must somehow remove or trim the size of report fields in order to make the report fit on a standard sheet of paper.

10. Suppose you decided that the History field should not be on the report. This information is not required on a customer directory.

    To remove this field, begin by placing your cursor on the History field. This field is at the extreme right end of the report design, marked by a long series of A's.

    Select the command:

    Menu [F10]/TableBand/Erase

11. A message at the top of the screen asks you to move to the column to be removed.

    Make sure the cursor is resting in the History field, the press **Enter**.

    Paradox removes the History column from the report design.

12. Move back to the beginning of the Table Band. To do this, press:

    [Ctrl-Home]

    The cursor jumps to the far left edge of the report specification.

    Notice the appearance of the Cust ID field. There is a lot of wasted space in this field because the column header is wider than the field it describes.

    You next rearrange the column to make it more compact.

13. Note the appearance of the column header, with the label "Cust ID" above a row of dashes.

    Position the cursor on top of the first dash in the Cust ID field. Insert a blank line at this position.

    To insert a blank row, press the **Insert** key to turn it on. When the Insert key is turned on, the cursor changes shape from a block to an underline.

    With the Insert key on, press **Enter**. Everything from the row of dashes and below moves downward one row.

14. The length of the Cust ID is only four characters. Using the **Del** key, remove all but four of the dashes in the field.

101

Now move to the label Cust ID. Edit this label to read:

Cust

ID

Your report design should look like this:

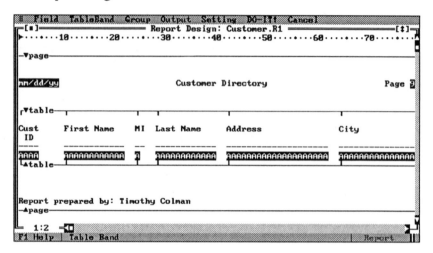

15. Next reduce the width of the column. Select the commands:

    Menu [F10]/TableBand/Resize

    Paradox displays a message asking you to move to the column you want to resize. It is important to position the cursor at the *right edge* of the column. If the cursor is left next to a field or a label, Paradox will not let you reduce the width of the column.

    Move the cursor to the right edge of the Cust ID column. Press **Enter**.

    The message on the screen asks you to use the arrow keys to adjust the size of the column. Press the **Left Arrow** until just two blank spaces are left in the column.

    Press **Enter** to complete the command.

16. Repeat this process for the **State** field. Recall the steps you just completed:

    • Edit the field labels. Delete extra characters and dashes.

    • Resize the column with the Menu [F10]/TableBand/Resize command. Remember to position the cursor at the right edge of the column.

    Use the following illustration to edit the field.

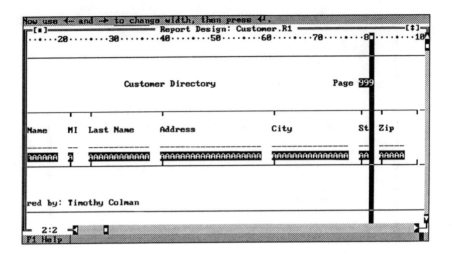

17. Even after this adjustment, the report is still too wide to fit within the margins of a standard 8.5" x 11" sheet of paper.

To make it fit, you trim the width of the Address and City fields. This involves the same steps described above, but in addition you must also trim the size of the data field in the report.

Trim the length of the Address field first. Move the cursor to the Address field.

18. Select the commands:

Menu [F10]/Field/Reformat

The Reformat option is used to change the display length of a field. It does not change the actual length of a field, only the amount of space it takes up on a report.

A message asks you to move onto the desired field. Place the cursor inside the "AAAAAAAAAAAAAAAAAAAAA" of the Address field.

Press **Enter.**

19. A message now asks you to use the arrow keys to adjust the size of the field.

Press the **Left Arrow** three times to trim this field by three spaces.

Press **Enter.** The field should now be three positions shorter than before.

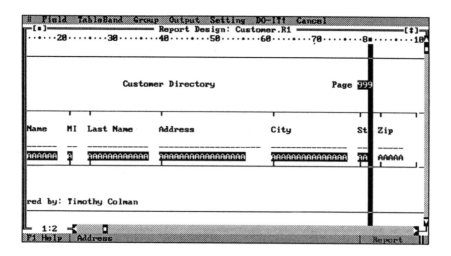

20. Now delete the three extra dashes above the Address field. Then use the **Menu [F10]/Field/Reformat** and the **Menu [F10]/TableBand/Resize** commands to reduce the width of the Address field.

    Trim this field to leave two blank spaces at the end.

    Finally, use the **Menu [F10]/TableBand/Resize** command to reduce the width of the City field. Trim this field by three spaces as you did with the Address field.

    Your screen now looks like the following illustration.

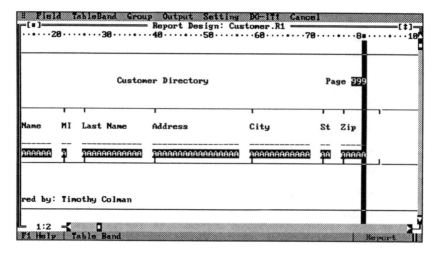

21. Next, send a test report to the screen. This allows you to review the appearance of the report before sending a copy to the printer.

    Select the commands:

    Menu [F10]/Output/Screen

    Paradox 4.5 sends a sample report to your screen. It should appear as shown below.

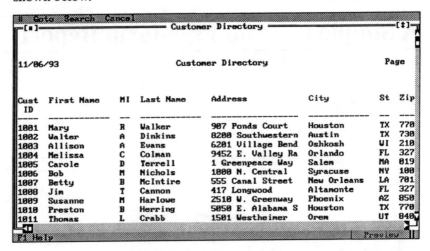

22. Note that when previewing the report you have a menu available to you. You can use the Goto option to look at a particular page of the report, or the Search option to locate a particular value in the report. Finally the Cancel option halts the preview.

    Select the **Cancel** option now by choosing:

    F10 [Report Preview menu]/Cancel/Yes

23. Paradox returns to the Report design screen. Save your report specification. Press the key:

    [F2] DO-IT!

    The report design is saved to disk, then Paradox returns to the desktop.

Section 35

A Simple Custom Free-form Report

In this exercise you build a simple customized report for the Inven table. This table captures information about your book inventory. When completed, your inventory report looks like this:

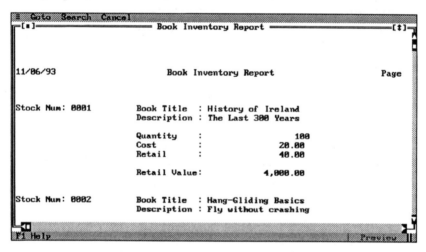

Notice that this report is arranged like a custom screen form. This is a *free-form* report. In a free-form report, you can position a field anywhere on the page. If you examine the screen closely, you will see a field not present in the table: Retail Value. This field is a *calculated* field. A calculated field is one which is based on the result of a calculation. To create the Retail Value field, you multiply the values in two fields: On-hand and Retail.

You now create the custom report.

1. Load the Inven table. Select the commands:

   Menu [F10]/View

   From the list of tables, select the **Inven** table. Take a moment to examine the table.

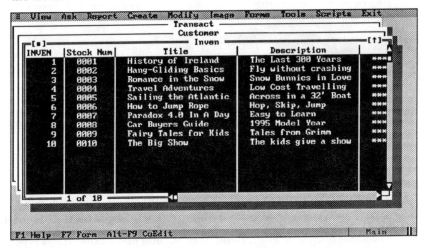

2. Now build a report for this table. Select the commands:

   Menu [F10]/Report

   Paradox displays a menu of reporting options. Select the option:

   Design

   When asked for a table name, select the **Inven** table.

3. Paradox displays a list of possible reports. As with custom forms, up to fifteen reports can be created for each table you define.

   Select report number **1**, the first unused report.

   When asked for a report description, type:

   Book Inventory Report

   Press **Enter**.

4. Paradox asks if you want a Tabular or Free-form report. Select:

   Free-form

   Paradox displays the report design screen, as shown on the following page.

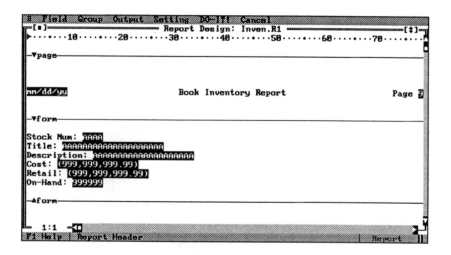

This free-form report design screen allows you to place data fields anywhere you want on the page.

5. As with the Tabular report, the report specification consists of bands. The upper Page Band contains information printed once at the top of the page.

The next band is the Form Band. Information in the Form Band is printed once for each record in the selected table, in this case the Inven table.

At the bottom of the screen is a second Page Band. This band contains information to be printed at the bottom of each page. The last portion of this Page Band is not visible at the bottom of the screen.

6. Compare the previous illustration with the one following. When complete, your custom report design should look like this:

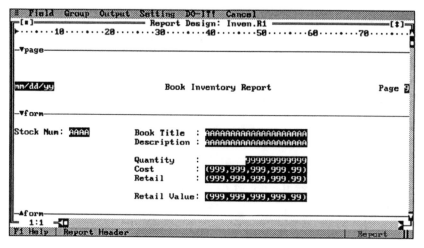

Notice that this report contains all of the fields from Inven plus a field not in the table: Retail Value. This field is calculated from data in the On-hand and the Retail fields.

7. Now begin building your report. Move the cursor down the screen into the Form Band. Place it in the left margin, on the "T" in Title.

   Delete the five rows containing the Title, Description, Cost, Retail, and On-hand fields. To delete a row, make sure the cursor is in the left margin of the screen. Press:

   [Ctrl-Y]

   This deletes the Title row. Press **[Ctrl-Y]** four more times. The remaining fields are deleted.

8. For the following steps, make sure the Insert key is turned on. If the Insert is on, the cursor appears as an underline rather than its normal block appearance.

   Notice the ruler line at the top of the screen. Use this ruler line to gauge your position on the screen.

9. Move the cursor to the same line as the Stock Num field. Position the cursor in column 25 on this line.

   Type the field label:

   Book Title :

   Press **Enter**.

   Notice the two spaces after the phrase Book Title and before the colon symbol. Be sure to include these spaces.

10. The cursor drops down to the next line of the Form Band. Because your Insert key was on, a line was inserted into the form band.

    Move the cursor to column 25, under the "B" in Book Title. Type:

    Description :

    Follow the word **Description** with one space. The colons from both labels should line up. Press **Enter**.

11. Add the remaining field labels to the form band. Remember to place blank lines and spaces where appropriate. Refer to the following illustration for help in positioning these labels.

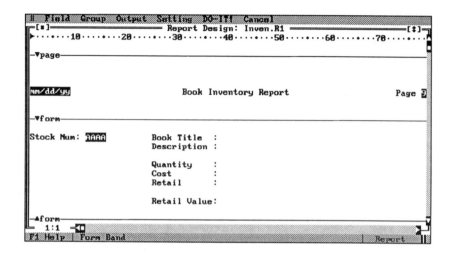

12. Now place the fields from the table on the report design. Move the cursor to the Book Title line, just to the *right* of the cursor.

    This should be about column 40 on the ruler line. Execute the command:

    Menu [F10]/Field/Place

    Paradox displays a menu with several field types. Most of your selections will be Regular. Select the option:

    Regular

13. Paradox shows a list of fields defined for the Inven table. Highlight the Title field, then press **Enter**.

    Paradox asks you to position the cursor at the beginning point for this field. The cursor should already be properly positioned. Press **Enter**.

14. Paradox now asks you to indicate the number of characters to print for this field. Pressing the **Left Arrow** would allow you to reduce the size of this field.

    Press **Enter** to accept the displayed field size.

    If you accidentally enter a blank line in your report format, remember to position the cursor on the blank line and in the left margin. Then use the [Ctrl-Y] command to delete this blank line.

15. Add the Description field next. Move the cursor to the Description row and under the beginning of the Title field.

    Select the commands:

    Menu [F10]/Field/Place/Regular

From the list of fields, choose **Description**. Position the cursor at the beginning point for the field and press **Enter**.

Note that the end of this field should match the end of the Title field in the line above it. If it does not match after you press **Enter**, then press the **Esc** key and Paradox will let you reposition the field.

After positioning the field, press **Enter** twice more to set the number of characters displayed for this field.

16. Repeat this process for the On-hand field. Move the cursor to the Quantity line. Select the commands:

    Menu [F10]/Field/Place/Regular

    From the list of fields, choose **On-hand**. Position the cursor at the beginning point for the field and press **Enter**.

    Follow the screen messages to adjust the number of positions to show for this field. Press **Enter** when done.

17. The next three fields are all fields that contain decimal places. This means that you will want to follow the screen messages closely. Be sure to include two decimal positions for this field in your screen definition.

    Move the cursor to the Cost line, then position it under the first digit of the Quantity field.

    At this point your report definition looks like this:

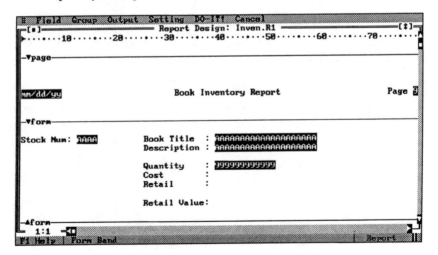

18. Select the commands:

    Menu [F10]/Field/Place/Regular

    From the list of fields, choose **Cost**. Since the cursor is already at the beginning point for the field, press **Enter**.

    Paradox asks you to adjust the number of positions to show. Leave the field size as displayed. Press **Enter**.

    Now Paradox asks to indicate the number of decimal places to show. Two decimals are displayed as a default. Keep this number. Press **Enter**.

19. Note the parentheses in the field description. These parentheses are only used by Paradox to denote negative numbers.

    Now place the Retail field on the report. Position the cursor opposite the field label, then select the command:

    Menu [F10]/Field/Place/Regular

    Follow the screen messages to adjust the number of positions and decimal places to show for this field. Press **Enter** when done.

20. Only one field remains, the Retail Value field. This field will be calculated as the On-hand field times the Retail field.

    Move the cursor to the Retail Value line and under the first character of the Retail field.

    Select the commands:

    Menu [F10]/Field/Place/Calculated

    Paradox displays a dialog box that asks you to enter an expression. Type:

    [On-hand]*[Retail]

    Be sure to include the square brackets in the expression. Press **Enter**.

21. Paradox asks you to position the field. Make sure the cursor is under the first parenthesis in the Retail field. Press **Enter**. Press **Enter** twice more to accept the number of digits and decimal positions to display.

    Your report format should look like the following illustration.

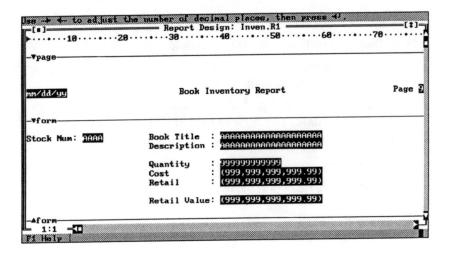

22. Send a sample report to the screen. Select the commands:

Menu [F10]/Output/Screen

Paradox prepares a sample report and sends it to the screen. Examine the appearance of the report, in particular the Quantity line. It appears too far to the left and does not line up at the right with the other numeric fields.

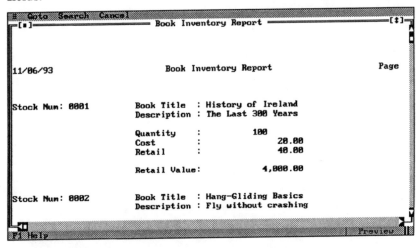

23. Press the **PgDn** key until you reach the end of the report. When ready, leave the report preview by selecting the commands:

Menu [F10]/Cancel/Yes

Paradox redisplays the report design screen.

24. Adjust the position of the On-hand field.

   When the report design screen reappears, position the cursor just in front of the On-hand field. Make sure the **Insert** key is turned on.

   Press the **Spacebar** to push the On-hand field to the right. Position it so that its last 9 digits line up with the last 9 of the Cost field.

25. Tell Paradox to save the report design. Press:

   DO-IT! [F2]

   Paradox saves the report design and returns to the Main mode.

Section 36

Printing the Custom Report

Once the custom report has been designed, it is very easy to print.

1. Select the commands:

   Menu [F10]/Report

   From the report options pull-down menu, select the option:

   Output

2. Paradox displays a dialog box asking for which table to generate a report. Press Enter to see a list of tables. From the list, select the **Inven** table.

   Paradox displays a list of reports for the Inven table. Highlight report number 1. Notice the report description to the left of the list: Book Inventory Report.

   Press **Enter** to select this report.

3. Paradox asks you for a destination for the report. Verify that the printer is online and ready. Select the **Printer** option and press **Enter**.

   Paradox prints a report like the one shown on the following page.

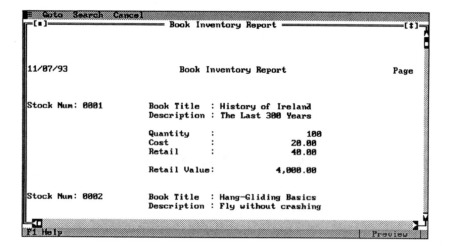

Section 37

Creating Simple Scripts in Paradox

Paradox defines a script as a record of the keys you press while carrying out commands. This record of keystrokes is saved and can be played back later much faster than from the keyboard. Scripts are ideal for those operations in Paradox you carry out repetitively. For example, you could create a script to load a table, create a query form for this table and execute it, then print a report for the resulting Answer table.

Once the script is created and saved, it can be easily replayed to carry out the same steps and produce the same report.

Paradox provides a pair of useful commands for creating and replaying scripts: Instant Script Record [Alt-F3] and Instant Script Play [Alt-F4].

In this example, you create a simple script to clear the desktop, load the Transact table, query the table, and print a standard report on the resulting Answer table.

1. Use the Instant Script Record command to create this script. Select the command:

   Instant Script Record [Alt-F3]

   Paradox displays the message "Begin recording of Instant..." in the message area at the lower right corner of the desktop. Notice also the letter R displayed at the far right of the Status Bar. This tells you that Paradox is recording your keystrokes. Each operation you carry out is stored in the script until you turn recording off.

2. Select the command:

   Clear All [Alt-F8]

   Paradox clears all tables from the desktop and displays the Main menu. This same command was also recorded in your script.

3. Select the command:

View

Select the **Transact** table. Paradox displays this table and continues recording your commands.

4. Now build and execute the query to extract order information for stock number 0005.

Select the commands:

Menu [F10]/Ask

Paradox asks you for a table name. Choose the **Transact** table. Paradox displays an empty query form in the desktop, as shown here.

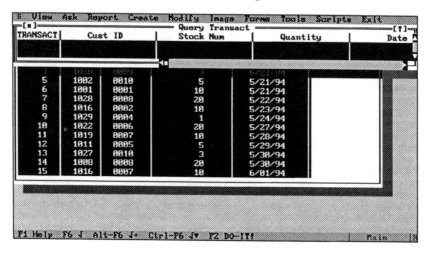

5. Fill out the query form. Place check marks in the Cust ID, Stock Num, Quantity, and Date fields using the command:

Checkmark [F6]

In addition, place the entry 0005 in the Stock Num column. This query asks the question "Which customers ordered stock number 0005, in what quantities and on what dates?"

Press:

DO-IT! [F2]

6. Paradox creates and displays the Answer table for this query, as shown in the following illustration.

Only one step remains: printing the standard report for the Answer table.

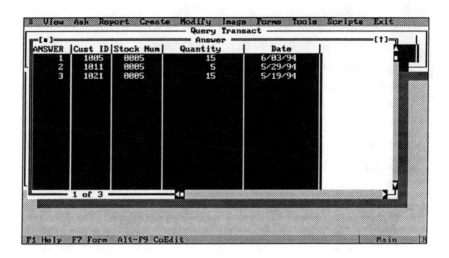

7. Make sure your printer is on-line and ready to go. Select the command:

Instant Report [Alt-F7]

Paradox creates and prints a standard report for the Answer table.

8. Now that you have completed the report, tell Paradox to stop recording your keystrokes.

To do this, use the Instant Script Record [Alt-F3] command again. This is another one of the Paradox toggle commands. The first time you execute this command, recording is turned on. The next time you execute the command, recording is turned off.

Press:

Instant Script Record [Alt-F3]

The letter R is removed from the lower right corner of the screen. Recording of keystrokes is stopped. The set of keystrokes you just recorded are saved on your disk under the name Instant.

9. Now play your script. Select the command:

Instant Script Play [Alt-F4]

Paradox executes the contents of your script and prints a second report for you.

Note that the screen does not change while the script is running. In order for the script to run as fast as possible, Paradox does not update the screen while the script runs. This does not mean it is not carrying out each step you included in the script, only that each step is not reflected on the screen. As soon as the script is complete, normal screen updates resume.

10. Because this is an Instant Script it will be written over the next time you execute the Instant Script Record command.

    We want to save this script so that we can display and edit it later. Execute these commands:

    Menu [F10]/Tools/Rename/Script

    Paradox 4.5 asks you for the current name of the script. Press the **Enter** key to display a list of available scripts.

11. Select the **Instant** script. Paradox now asks you for the new name for your script.

    Type a new name for your script:

    STOCKNUM

    Press **Enter**. This preserves your instant script under the new name STOCKNUM. You may now record a new instant script without overwriting the one you just created.

Section 38

Graphics in Paradox

Paradox can create and display information from tables in on-screen graphs. You can quickly display a graph for the current table using the Instant Graph [Ctrl-F7] command.

Paradox provides a set of graph commands that allow you to create custom graphs of several kinds. These commands are selected with the Menu [F10]/Image/Graph command.

In this exercise, you create a simple graph for the Inven table.

1. Bring the Inven table to the screen. Select the commands:

   Menu [F10]/View

   Press **Enter** to display a list of table names. Select the **Inven** table. Paradox displays a table like this one:

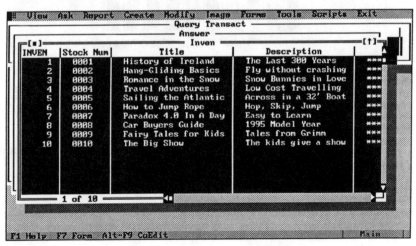

2. The Inven table contains an On-hand field showing the amount of each title on hand in your warehouse.

   Suppose you would like to see a graph of the number of each stock number on hand in the warehouse.

   This can be done easily with the Instant Graph [Ctrl-F7] command.

3. Move the cursor to the On-hand column of the Inven table. This is the column we want Paradox to build into the graph.

   Now tell Paradox to create a graph. Select the command:

   Instant Graph [Ctrl-F7]

   Paradox creates and displays a graph of the Inven table, as shown below.

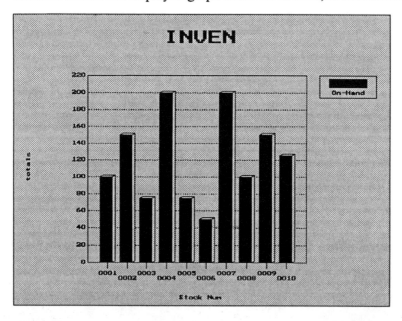

   When done viewing the graph, press the Spacebar to return to the Table view.

4. What if you want to modify the appearance of the graph? Let's modify the appearance of the graph to a pie chart.

   Select the commands:

   Menu [F10]/Image/Graph/Modify

   Paradox displays a graphics options screen, as shown here.

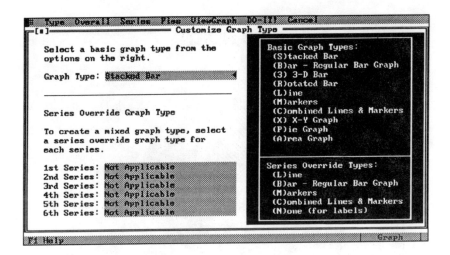

5. Now modify the graph type.

   Notice the box labeled "Basic Graph Types" in the upper right corner. It lists ten different graph types. You can select the first letter of the graph type to make it the new graph type.

   Type the letter:

   P

   Paradox displays a new graph type: Pie.

6. Tell Paradox to complete the changes to the graph. Select the command:

   DO-IT! [F2]

   Paradox saves the changes to the graph type, then returns to the desktop.

7. Redisplay the graph, this time as a Pie chart. Select the command:

   Instant Graph [Ctrl-F7]

   Paradox recreates and displays a graph of the Inven table, this time as a pie chart as shown on the following page.

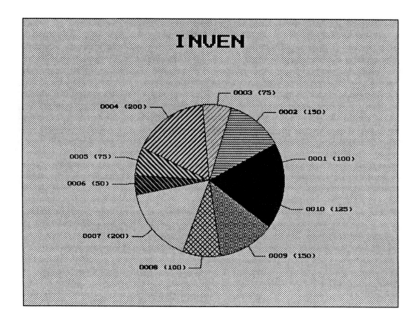

When done viewing the graph, press the **Spacebar** to return to the Table view.

Index

Other Books from Wordware Publishing, Inc.

Popular Applications Series (cont.)
Learn Microsoft Word 6.0 for
    Windows in a Day
Learn Microsoft Works in a Day
Learn Microsoft Works 3.0 in a Day
Learn Microsoft Works 3.0 for
    Windows in a Day
Learn Norton Utilities in a Day
Learn Novell NetWare Software
    in a Day
Learn OS/2 in a Day
Learn PageMaker 4.0 in a Day
Learn PageMaker 5.0 in a Day
Learn PAL in a Day
Learn PAL 4.5 in a Day
Learn Paradox 4.0 in a Day
Learn Paradox 4.5 in a Day
Learn Pascal in Three Days
Learn PC-Tools 8.0 in a Day
Learn PlanPerfect in a Day
Learn Q&A 4.0 in a Day
Learn Quattro Pro 4.0 in a Day
Learn Quattro Pro 5.0 in a Day
Learn Quicken in a Day
Learn Timeslips for Windows in a Day
Learn Turbo Assembler
    Programming in a Day
Learn Ventura 4.0 in a Day
Learn Windows in a Day
Learn Windows NT in a Day
Learn Word 2.0 for Windows in a Day
Learn WordPerfect in a Day
    (2nd Edition)
Learn WordPerfect 6.0 in a Day
Learn WordPerfect 5.2 for Windows
    in a Day
Learn WordPerfect 6.0 for Windows
    in a Day
Learn WordPerfect Presentations
    in a Day
Moving from WordPerfect for DOS to
    WordPerfect for Windows
Object-Oriented Programming using
    Turbo C++

Popular Applications Series (cont.)
Programming Output Drivers using
    Borland C++
Repair and Upgrade Your Own PC
WordPerfect 6.0 Survival Skills
Write TSRs Now
Write Your Own Programming
    Language using C++

At A Glance Series
CorelDRAW! for Windows
    at a Glance
FoxPro 2.5 at a Glance
FoxPro for Windows at a Glance
Lotus 1-2-3 Rel. 4 for Windows
    at a Glance
Microsoft Excel 5.0 for Windows
    at a Glance
Microsoft Visual Basic 3.0 for
    Windows at a Glance
Microsoft Windows at a Glance
Microsoft Word 6.0 for Windows
    at a Glance
Paradox 4.5 at a Glance
Quattro Pro 5.0 at a Glance
Quattro Pro 4.0 for Windows
    at a Glance
Quattro Pro 5.0 for Windows
    at a Glance
Word 2.0 for Windows at a Glance
WordPerfect 6.0 at a Glance
WordPerfect 6.0 for Windows
    at a Glance

**Hands-on Windows Programming
Series**
1   Introduction to Window
     Programming
2   Child Windows
3   Painting the Screen
4   Transferring Data To and From
     Windows

Call Wordware Publishing, Inc. for names of the bookstores in your area
(214) 423-0090

Other Books from Wordware Publishing, Inc.

Illustrated Series

Illustrated AutoCAD (Release 10)
Illustrated C Programming (ANSI)
(2nd Ed.)
Illustrated DacEasy Accounting 4.2
Illustrated dBASE III Plus
Illustrated dBASE IV 1.1
Illustrated MS-DOS 5.0
Illustrated Novell NetWare
2.x/3.x Software
Illustrated PageMaker 4.0
Illustrated Q&A 4.0
Illustrated QBasic for MS-DOS 5.0
Illustrated UNIX System V
Illustrated WordPerfect 5.1
Illustrated WordPerfect for Windows

General and Advanced Topics

111 Clipper Functions
The Complete Communications
Handbook
Financial Modeling using Lotus 1-2-3
Graphic User Interface Programming
with C
Graphics Programming with Turbo
Pascal
Novell NetWare: Advanced
Techniques and Applications
Programming On-Line Help
using C++
Understanding 3COM Networks

Advanced Networking Series

Demystifying SNA
Demystifying TCP/IP
Integrating TCP/IP into SNA
Networking with Windows NT

Popular Applications Series

Build Your Own Computer
Cost Control Using Lotus 1-2-3
Desktop Publishing Handbook
Desktop Publishing with Microsoft
Word 6.0 for Windows

Popular Applications Series (cont.)

Desktop Publishing with Word 2.0
for Windows
Desktop Publishing with WordPerfect
Desktop Publishing with WordPerfect
for Windows
Developing and Distributing
Microsoft FoxPro 2.5 for Windows
Applications
Developing Utilities in Assembly
Language
Learn AmiPro 3.0 in a Day
Learn AutoCAD in a Day
Learn AutoCAD 12 in a Day
Learn AutoCAD LT for Windows
in a Day
Learn C in Three Days
Learn dBASE Programming in a Day
Learn DOS in a Day
Learn DOS 6.0 in a Day
Learn DOS 6.2 in a Day
Learn DrawPerfect in a Day
Learn Excel for Windows
in a Day (Ver. 3.0 & 4.0)
Learn FoxPro 2.5 for Windows
in a Day
Learn Freelance Graphics for
Windows in a Day
Learn Generic CADD 6.0 in a Day
Learn Harvard Graphics 3.0 in a Day
Learn Lotus 1-2-3 in a Day
(Ver. 2.0-2.4)
Learn Lotus 1-2-3 Rel. 4 for
Windows in a Day
Learn Lotus 1-2-3 Rel. 4 for DOS
in a Day
Learn MS Access 2.0 for Windows
in a Day
Learn Microsoft Assembler in a Day
Learn Microsoft Excel 5.0 for
Windows in a Day
Learn Microsoft FoxPro 2.5 in a Day
Learn Microsoft PowerPoint 4.0
for Windows in a Day
Learn Microsoft Publisher 2.0
for Windows in a Day

Call Wordware Publishing, Inc. for names of the bookstores in your area
(214) 423-0090